MW01010085

SIMPLY
Scrappy Quilts

That
Patchwork
Place

Acknowledgments

Special thanks are extended to:

Heirloom Quilts, Poulsbo, Washington, for maintaining a wonderful assortment of fabrics to inspire me;

Carol Dunklau and Lonnie Henderson, for providing quilts;

Jo Baxter, Sharyn Squier Craig, Judy Martin, and Paulette Peters, for use of their designs;

Mrs. Eli Barkman, Donna K. Gundlach, Clara Hershberger, Mrs. Dan R. Miller, Hazel Montague, Alvina Nelson, Nancy Sweeney, Alma Troyer, Sue von Jentzen, Mrs. Abe Yoder, and Mrs. Andy A. Yoder, for their fine quilting;

Cherry and Terry Jarvis, for the loan of their beach cottage and props for photography;

Cleo Nollette, for her generous help in cutting, stitching, illustrating, and pattern testing.

Credits

Technical Editor .... Laura M. Reinstatler
Managing Editor .... Greg Sharp
Illustrator .... Brian Metz
Illustration Assistant .... Lisa McKenney
Copy Editor .... Tina Cook
Text Designer .... Sandy Wing
Cover Designer .... Cheryl Stevenson
Design Director .... Judy Petry
Production Assistant .... Claudia L'Heureux
Proofreaders .... Leslie Phillips
                                                            Melissa Riesland
Photographer .... Brent Kane
Photography Assistant .... Richard Lipshay

MISSION STATEMENT

WE ARE DEDICATED TO PROVIDING QUALITY PRODUCTS THAT ENCOURAGE CREATIVITY AND PROMOTE SELF-ESTEEM IN OUR CUSTOMERS AND OUR EMPLOYEES.

WE STRIVE TO MAKE A DIFFERENCE IN THE LIVES WE TOUCH.

That Patchwork Place is an employee-owned, financially secure company.

Simply Scrappy Quilts
©1995 by Nancy J. Martin

That Patchwork Place, Inc.
PO Box 118
Bothell, WA 98041-0118 USA

Printed in Hong Kong
00 99 98 97 96   6 5 4 3 2

No part of this product may be reproduced in any form, unless otherwise stated, in which case reproduction is limited to the use of the purchaser. The written instructions, photographs, designs, projects, and patterns are intended for the personal noncommercial use of the retail purchaser and are under federal copyright laws; they are not to be reproduced by any electronic, mechanical, or other means, including informational storage or retrieval systems, for commercial use.

The information in this book is presented in good faith, but no warranty is given nor results guaranteed. Since That Patchwork Place, Inc., has no control over choice of materials or procedures, the company assumes no responsibility for the use of this information.

Library of Congress Cataloging-in-Publication Data
Martin, Nancy J.
        Simply scrappy quilts / Nancy J. Martin.
            p. cm.
        ISBN 1-56477-127-X
        1. Patchwork—Patterns. 2. Patchwork quilts. 3. Rotary cutting.
I. Title.
TT835.M2734 1995
746.46—dc20
                                                                                            95-43744
                                                                                                    CIP

Contents

Introduction

Literally and historically, the words "scrap quilt" refer to a quilt that has been made from leftover fabric and worn, discarded textile scraps. During the late nineteenth century, when most women had to produce all of the family's clothing and linens, leftover pieces of homespun, linen, and dressmaking scraps were used in the utility quilts of that era. The "good" fabric left from worn or outgrown clothing was collected with leftover scraps in a scrap bag. When utility quilts were needed for bedding, the scrap bag was brought out, and these textiles were stitched into a quilt. It often took a long time to use up all the fabric in a scrap bag, so some antique quilts contain fabrics that were manufactured during a span of thirty to forty years.

The traditional scrap bag is a thing of the past; today's scrap bag contains new fabrics left over from planned quilt projects. Today's quilter may recycle newspapers, cans, plastic bottles, and miscellaneous paper, but rarely fabric. She buys more fabric and delights as it accumulates.

"Scrap quilt" now refers to a color recipe that uses an assortment of light and dark fabrics. These quilts are characterized by exuberant color schemes, lively combinations of fabrics, and random pattern placement. Many quilters buy new fabrics to use in their scrap quilts. Of course, the more frugal among us try to utilize leftover fabrics, but the temptation to buy new fabric is quite strong and usually prevails.

As I began assembling quilt plans, sketches, and fabric swatches for my twenty-sixth book, I was struck by the number of designs that I intended to make as scrap quilts. I have always preferred to make my quilts using a combination of fabrics that are similar in color and value, rather than using only one fabric for the background, another single fabric for the dark, and one more for the accent. "Fabric Selection" on pages 15–16 gives some general guidelines for planning scrap quilts.

A scrap quilt color scheme offers several benefits over the more traditional two- or three-fabric approach.

- You can use leftover fabric, extra strips, and pieced units from other quilting projects.
- It's easy to substitute a look-alike if you run short of a fabric.
- Scrap quilts can grow into larger sizes as you stitch, since it is not necessary to use the exact fabrics you used at the beginning of the project.

The "Leftovers" section on pages 94–101 will help you cope with leftover fabric and bias squares. It features projects in a variety of sizes, ranging from pillows to full-size quilts.

For added inspiration, there is a gallery of color photographs that shows these wonderful scrappy quilts in room settings. These quilts are meant to be used and displayed, for they add warmth and charm to a home.

Now is the time to get out that bag of scraps, select one of the twenty-one designs found in this book, and experience the fun of making a Simply Scrappy quilt.

Nancy J. Martin

About the Author

Nancy J. Martin, talented author, teacher and quiltmaker, has written more than 25 books on quiltmaking. Nancy is an innovator in the quilting industry and introduced the Bias Square® cutting ruler to quilters everywhere. Along with more than 18 years of teaching experience and numerous classic quilting titles to her credit, Nancy is the founder and President of That Patchwork Place, Inc., the publisher of America's Best-Loved Quilt Books™. Nancy and her husband Dan enjoy living in the Pacific Northwest.

► *The bold color schemes in CITY LIGHTS on the bed and ELECTRIC SKY on the wall energize this bedroom.*

Gallery

▲ *French fabrics purchased at*
Le Rouvray in Paris are used
in this sophisticated
EVENING IN PARIS quilt.

▶ *Reproduction 1930s fabrics are*
combined with authentic 1930s fabrics
in the ROAD TO OKLAHOMA quilt
and pillows on the bed.

◀ *WONDERFUL WORLD, made with*
bright, clear colors, repeats the floral
fabric used on the sofa and chair.
A scrappy OCEAN WAVES quilt,
folded over the arm of the chair,
is just right for napping.

▲ *VINTAGE WINE is the focal point of this sewing room wall.*

◄ *Romantic and feminine, BUTTONS AND BOWS hangs on the wall of this old-fashioned country cottage.*

► *This welcoming guest room displays two quilts that feature an assortment of pink fabrics: ROSY RASPBERRY on the wall and SWEETNESS AND LIGHT on the bed.*

▲ *FREE TRADE, made from a variety of navy blue fabrics, is surrounded by lighthouse and sailboat memorabilia.*

◄ *A rustic country birdhouse rests on the SCRAPPY STAR quilt below GOING TO MEETING.*

◄◄ *Scrappy quilts are the perfect addition to this rustic country cabin. FRIENDSHIP STAR and DUTCHMAN'S PUZZLE hang on a twig quilt rack near LOVE CHAIN on the bed.*

Rotary Cutter and Mat

A large rotary cutter enables you to quickly cut strips and pieces without templates. A cutting mat is essential to protect both the blade and table on which you are cutting. An 18" x 24" mat allows you to cut long strips, on the straight or bias grain. You might also consider purchasing a smaller mat to use when working with scraps.

Use a clear acrylic ruler to measure fabric and guide the rotary cutter. It is possible to cut quilt pieces with any see-through ruler that you have, and you can also adapt a general-purpose ruler to cut bias squares. It is easier, however, to use the special rulers that I recommend. They contain only the cutting lines and strategic alignment guides necessary to keep the fabric grain line in the correct position. Since you don't have to visually screen out unnecessary lines, your eyes can quickly focus on only the lines you need. Using a specialized ruler improves cutting accuracy, makes quiltmaking more fun, and frees you from the matching and stitching frustrations that can result from inaccurate cuts.

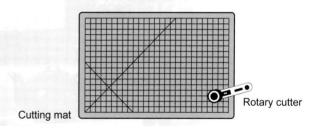

Cutting mat   Rotary cutter

Rotary-Cutting Rulers

Use a see-through ruler to measure and guide the rotary cutter. There are many appropriate rulers on the market, but my favorite is the Rotary Rule™. It is 24" long and is made from 1/8"-thick clear Plexiglas®. It includes markings for 45° and 60° angles, guidelines for cutting strips, and standard measurements. The Rotary Mate™ is a 12"-long ruler with the same features. Both of these rulers are marked with large, clear numbers and do not have a lot of confusing lines.

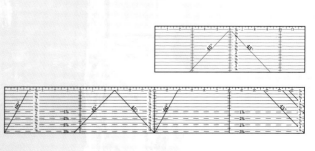

◄ *CHRISTMAS WREATH hangs on the wall and FRIENDSHIP STAR is draped over the wagon. Together they announce the coming holiday season.*

The Bias Square® ruler is critical for cutting accurate bias squares. This acrylic ruler is available in three sizes: 4", 6", or 8" square, and is ruled with $\frac{1}{8}$" markings. It features a diagonal line, which is placed on the bias seam, enabling you to cut two accurately sewn half-square triangles.

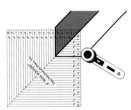

The Bias Square is also convenient to use when cutting small quilt pieces, such as squares, rectangles, and triangles. The larger 8" size is ideal for quick-cutting blocks that require large squares and triangles as well as for making diagonal cuts for half-square and quarter-square triangles. A 20cm-square metric version is also available.

If these rulers are not available at your local quilt or fabric shop, they can be ordered from That Patchwork Place, Inc., P.O. Box 118, Bothell, WA 98041-0118.

If the Bias Square is unavailable, you can adapt a general-purpose rotary ruler to work in a similar fashion.

1. Make a template by cutting a square of see-through plastic in the size specified for the bias square in the quilt directions.
2. Draw a diagonal line on the template, bisecting the square.
3. Tape the template to the corner of an acrylic ruler.
4. Follow the cutting directions given for the quilt you are making, substituting the template-adapted corner of the ruler for the Bias Square.

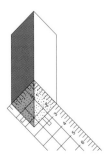

You will need to make a new template for each size bias square required for the quilt you are making. The most common sizes of bias squares are 2", $2\frac{1}{2}$", and 3".

Sewing Machine

Stitching quilts on a sewing machine is easy and enjoyable. Spend some time getting to know your machine and become comfortable with its use. Keep your machine dust-free and well oiled.

Machine piecing does not require an elaborate sewing machine. All you need is a straight-stitch machine in good working order. It should make an evenly locked straight stitch that looks the same on both sides of the seam. Adjust the tension, if necessary, to produce smooth, even seams. A puckered seam causes the fabric to curve, distorting the size and shape of the piecing and the quilt you are making.

Pins

A good supply of glass- or plastic-headed pins is necessary. Long pins are especially helpful when pinning thick layers together.

If you plan to machine quilt, you will need to hold the layers of the quilt together with a large supply of rustproof, size 2 safety pins.

Iron and Ironing Board

Frequent and careful pressing is necessary to ensure a smooth, accurately stitched quilt top. Place your iron and ironing board, along with a plastic spray bottle of water, close to your sewing machine.

Needles

Use sewing-machine needles sized for cotton fabrics (size 70/10 or 80/12). You also need hand-sewing needles (Sharps) and hand-quilting needles (Betweens #8, #9, and #10).

Scissors

Use good-quality shears, and use them only for cutting fabric. Thread snips or embroidery scissors are handy for clipping stray threads.

Seam Ripper

This little tool will come in handy if you find it necessary to remove a seam before resewing.

Some quilt patterns in this book call for an assortment of light and dark fabrics, others for a combination of lights, accents, and darks. Your fabric and color choices will depend on what appeals to you, what is available in your scrap bag, or what fat quarters or fat eighths you have purchased.

If you have trouble deciding on a color scheme, select a color-coordinated bundle of fat quarters or fat eighths. Often, this can be the basis for an effective color scheme with the purchase of additional background fabric. You can also purchase more of a particular fabric that you wish to predominate in your quilt. For instance, if the fabric requirements call for six dark fat quarters, you can purchase three fat quarters of a red print that you really like and one fat quarter of each of three other red prints.

Many of the quilts shown in this book do not use a single light print as a background print but a combination of fabrics that are similar in color and value. Study the differences in these quilts and see which you prefer. If you prefer the look of a single light background fabric, convert yardage given in fat quarters to yards. To do so, divide the number of fat quarters by four. For example, fourteen fat quarters equals 3½ yards of fabric.

For best results, select lightweight, closely woven, 100% cotton fabrics. Fabrics with a polyester content may make small patchwork pieces difficult to cut and sew accurately.

Wash all fabrics first to preshrink, test for colorfastness, and get rid of excess dye. Continue to wash fabric until the rinse water is completely clear. Add a square of white fabric to each washing of the fabric. When this white fabric remains its original color, the fabric is colorfast. A cupful of vinegar in the rinse water can also be used to help set difficult dyes.

After washing, press fabric and fold into fourths lengthwise. Make straight cuts with the rotary cutter across each end. When using the length of fabric, make straight cuts from one end and bias cuts from the other end. Then fold the fabric to store it.

Make it a habit to wash and prepare fabrics after you purchase them. Then your fabric will be ready to sew when you are.

YARDAGE REQUIREMENTS

As a quilting teacher, I have often seen the problems created by purchasing too little fabric. There is no flexibility to make the quilt bigger, to make a mistake, or to change your mind. So the fabric requirements given in this book are generous and based on yardage that is 42" wide after prewashing. If your fabric is wider than 42", there will be a little left over at the end of your strips. If your fabric is narrower than 42", you may need to cut an extra strip. Save any extra yardage or strips for future scrap quilts. (See "Leftovers" on pages 94–101.)

Many of the yardage amounts in this book specify fat quarters. This is an 18" x 22" piece of fabric rather than the standard quarter-yard that is cut selvage to selvage and measures 9" x 44". The fat quarter is a more convenient size to use, especially when cutting bias strips for bias squares. Another common size is the fat eighth, which measures 9" x 22". Shops often offer the added convenience of fat quarters and fat eighths already cut and bundled. Look for the basket or bin of fat quarters and fat eighths when selecting fabrics.

FABRIC PLACEMENT

First look to see if your quilt pattern has a "background" on which a design will appear. Most quilts do. If so, select your background fabric first. Don't limit your choices to solid colors, even though muslin is a traditional background fabric for scrap quilts. If you really want to use a solid-colored fabric, try a deep turkey red or perhaps black or navy blue for an Amish look. Remember, solid-colored fabrics tend to emphasize mismatched seams and irregular quilting stitches. If you are a beginner and are still perfecting your piecing and quilting skills, select a print that is more likely to hide minor imperfections.

Choose a background print that is nondirectional and still appears unified after being cut apart and resewn. Study the examples on the next page for good and poor choices of background fabric.

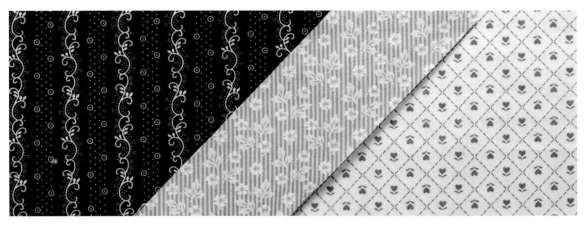

Unsuitable background fabrics

Suitable background fabrics

To test the suitability of background fabrics while shopping, make several directional folds and evaluate the unity of the design.

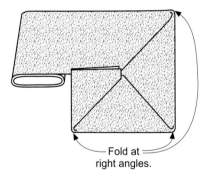

Fold at right angles.

Prints with a white background have a clean, formal look; those with a beige or tan background resemble antique quilts and have a more informal look.

Once you have chosen the background fabric, select the remaining fabrics that will enhance the background fabric. Study the colors in the background-fabric design and begin your selection. If working with a single color family, such as blue, select a wide range of blue fabrics. Begin with deep, dark navy blues, adding royal blues, medium blues, and light blues. If most of your blue fabrics are bright, stick to bright blues in all shades. If your blue fabrics are dull or "grayed," select muted shades of blue fabrics. Study the photo of "Going to Meeting" on page 51 to see the wide range of blue fabrics selected.

If you work with scraps or fat quarters, you will use a number of different fabrics to represent a single value. When cutting the pieces shown as dark in the quilt plan, for example, you can use two, three, or ten different dark fabrics. These might all be the same color (such as an assortment of reds) or different colors of the same value (such as a combination of dark blues, dark greens, and browns).

If you are using fabric randomly, don't worry about the placement of stripes or plaids. Let them fall as they are cut, including off-grain plaids. Stripes can be used both horizontally and vertically in the same block.

Controlling the direction of striped fabric or directional prints requires careful cutting and place-ment. For example, in cutting half-square triangles, cut half the triangles in one direction and the remaining triangles in the opposite direction.

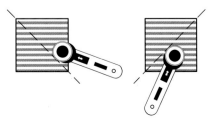

When sewing these pieces to a square or diamond, stitch the triangles from squares cut in one direction to opposite sides of the center square.

Then sew the pieces from squares cut in the opposite direction to the remaining sides of the center square.

To center a design from a pictorial or theme print, use a see-through ruler and adjust the crosswise cuts to center the design.

COMMON QUILT TERMS

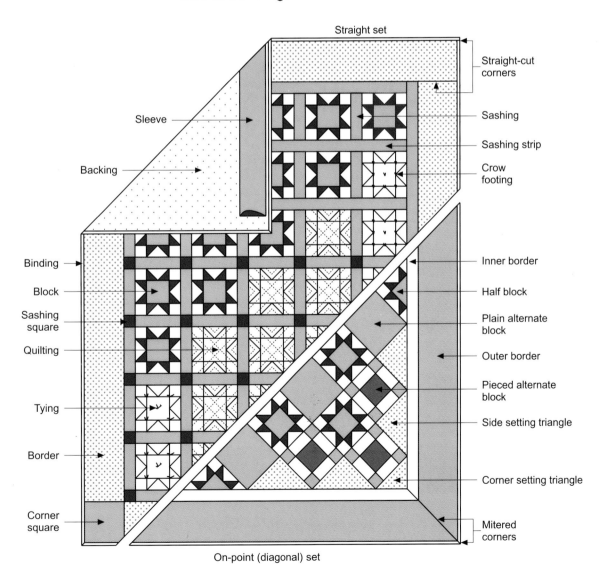

Straight set

Straight-cut corners

Sleeve

Sashing

Sashing strip

Backing

Crow footing

Binding

Inner border

Block

Half block

Sashing square

Plain alternate block

Quilting

Outer border

Pieced alternate block

Tying

Side setting triangle

Border

Corner setting triangle

Corner square

Mitered corners

On-point (diagonal) set

USE AND CARE OF A ROTARY CUTTER

A rotary cutter has a *very sharp* blade. It is so sharp that you can cut yourself without even knowing it. If you are not extremely careful, you can also cut other people and objects that you had no intention of slicing. Before you use your rotary cutter for the first time, it is important to know some simple safety rules.

- Close the safety shield when the rotary cutter is not in use.
- Roll the cutter away from yourself. Plan the cutting so your fingers, hands, and arms are never at risk.
- Keep the cutter out of the reach of children.
- Dispose of used blades in a responsible manner. Wrap and tape cardboard around them before placing them in the garbage.

For comfort's sake, think about your posture and the table height as you cut. Stand to cut—you'll have more control than when sitting. Many quilters find they are more comfortable and can work longer if the cutting table is higher than a normal sewing table, so they don't have to bend as they cut. If you work on a table that is placed away from a wall, you can easily walk to another side of the table to make your next cut, rather than moving the fabric or the cutting mat.

If you are left-handed, reverse all cutting directions.

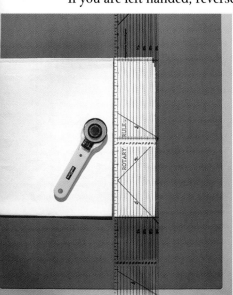

Begin by placing the fabric to your left and the ruler to your right. Use a mirror to view the photos. This will help you see the proper cutting alignment.

Remove the lint that builds up between the blade and the front sheath of your rotary cutter. Dismantle the cutter, paying close attention to how the pieces go together. Carefully wipe the blade with a soft, clean cloth, adding a small drop of sewing-machine oil to the blade where it lies under the front sheath. Try this before changing to a new blade when the cutting action seems dull.

GRAIN LINES

Fabric is made of threads (called yarns) that are woven together at right angles. This gives fabric the ability to stretch or remain stable, depending on the grain line you use. The lengthwise grain runs parallel to the selvage and has little stretch, while the crosswise grain runs from selvage to selvage and has some give to it. Lines drawn at angles to the straight grain lines are considered bias. A true bias is a line that runs at a 45° angle to the lengthwise and crosswise grains.

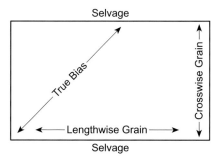

In most cases, the rotary-cutting directions use the following guides for grain-line placement:

- All strips are cut on the crosswise grain of fabric.
- Squares and rectangles are cut on the lengthwise and crosswise grains of fabric.
- Half-square triangles are cut with the short sides on the straight grain and the long side on the bias. The Bias Square technique produces sewn half-square triangles whose grain lines follow this guideline.
- Quarter-square triangles have the short sides on the bias and the long side on the straight grain. They are generally used along the outside edges of the quilt, where the long edge will not stretch.
- The straight grain of fabric should fall on the outside edge of all pieced blocks.

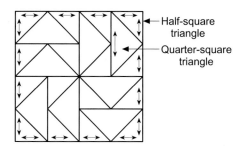

If fabric is badly off-grain, pull diagonally to straighten as shown.

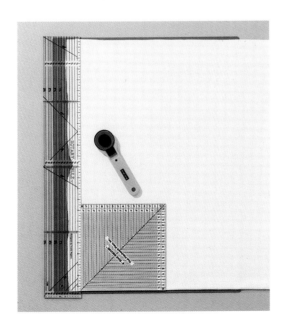

Since many fabrics are printed off-grain, it is impossible to rotary cut fabrics exactly on the straight grain of fabric. In rotary cutting, straight, even cuts are made as close to the grain as possible. A slight variation from the grain will not alter your project.

CUTTING STRAIGHT STRIPS

Rotary cutting squares, rectangles, and other shapes begins with cutting strips of fabric. These strips are then crosscut to the proper dimensions. All strip measurements include 1/4"-wide seam allowances.

To cut strips from the crosswise grain:

1. Fold and press the fabric with selvages matching, aligning the crosswise and lengthwise grains as much as possible. Place the folded fabric on the rotary-cutting mat, with the folded edge closest to your body. Align the Bias Square with the fold of the fabric and place a ruler to the left as shown.

2. Remove the Bias Square and make a rotary cut along the right side of the ruler to square up the edge of the fabric. Hold the ruler down with your left hand, placing the smallest finger off the edge of the ruler to serve as an anchor and prevent slipping. Stand comfortably, with your head and body centered over your cutting. Do not twist your body or arm into an awkward position.

As you cut, carefully reposition your hand on the ruler to make sure the ruler doesn't shift and the markings remain accurately placed. Use firm, even pressure as you cut. Begin rolling the cutter on the mat before you reach the folded fabric edge and continue across. For safety's sake, always roll the cutter away from you. Remember that the blade is very sharp, so be careful!

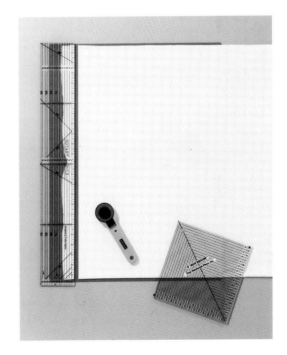

3. Fold the fabric again so that you will be cutting four layers at a time. Cut strips of fabric, aligning the clean-cut edge of the fabric with the ruler markings at the desired width. Open the fabric strips periodically to make sure you are cutting straight strips. If the strips are not straight, use the Bias Square to realign the ruler on the folded fabric, and make a fresh cut as in steps 1 and 2 to square up the edge of the fabric before cutting additional strips. Don't worry. This adjustment is common.

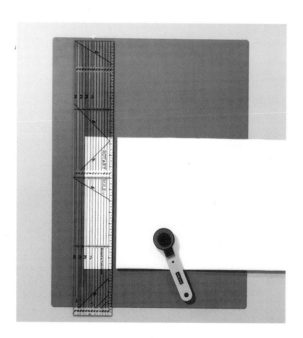

SQUARES AND RECTANGLES

1. Cut fabric into strips the measurement of the finished square plus seam allowances.

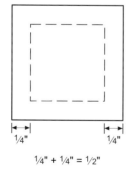

1/4"   1/4"

1/4" + 1/4" = 1/2"

2. Using the Bias Square, align the top and bottom edges of the strip and cut the fabric into squares the width of the strip.

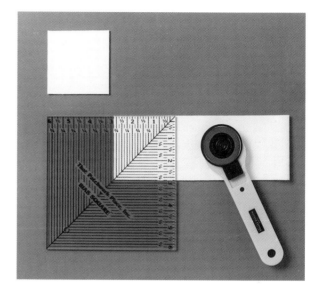

3. Cut rectangles in the same manner. First use the shorter measurement of the rectangle to cut strips, then use the longer measurement to cut the strips into rectangles.

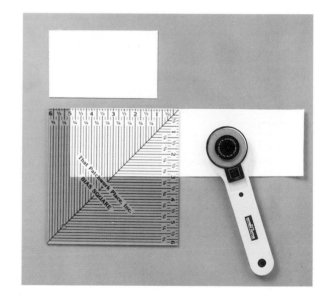

4. To cut a small, odd-sized square or rectangle for which there is no marking on your cutting guide, make an accurate paper template (including 1/4"-wide seam allowances). Tape it to the bottom of the Bias Square, and you will have the correct alignment for cutting strips or squares.

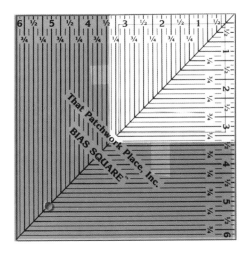

HALF-SQUARE TRIANGLES

Most of the triangles used in the quilts in this book are half-square triangles. These triangles are cut so that the straight grain is on the short edges of the triangle. Cut a square 7/8" larger than the finished size of the short edge of the triangle to allow for seam allowances; then cut the square once diagonally to yield two half-square triangles.

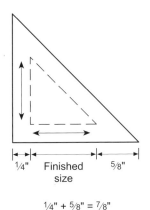

1/4" + 5/8" = 7/8"

1. Add 7/8" to the desired finished size and cut a strip to this measurement.
2. Cut the strip into squares, the same measurement as the strip width.

3. Cut a stack of squares once diagonally.

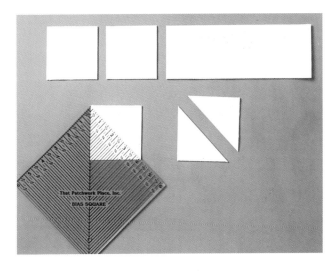

Nubbing Corners on Half-Square Triangles

Nubbing the corners on half-square triangles makes it easier to match edges precisely. Use the Bias Square to trim the corners. The example shown here is a half-square triangle with a finished dimension of 4".

1. To quick-cut this triangle, cut a 4⅞" square of fabric; then cut it once diagonally.
2. To trim the corners, add 1/2" to the finished size of the short side. Position the Bias Square's 4½" mark on the fabric triangle as shown. The points of the triangle will extend 3/8". Trim them off with the rotary cutter.

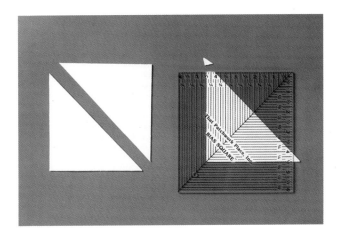

QUARTER-SQUARE TRIANGLES

These triangles are cut so that the straight grain is on the long edges of the triangles. The long sides are placed along the outside edges of blocks and quilts to keep the edges of quilts from stretching. Cut a square 1¼" larger than the finished size of the long edge of the triangle; then cut it twice diagonally to yield four quarter-square triangles.

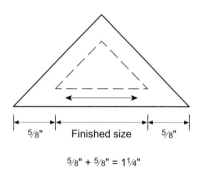

| ⅝" | Finished size | ⅝" |

⅝" + ⅝" = 1¼"

1. Cut a strip as wide as the desired finished measurement plus 1¼".
2. Cut the strip into squares that are the same measurement as the strip width.
3. Cut a stack of squares twice diagonally.

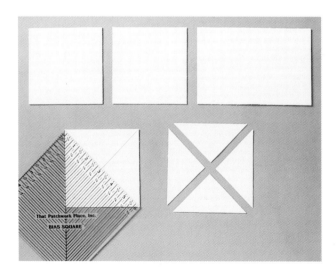

CUTTING BIAS STRIPS

To cut bias strips for binding:

1. Align the 45° marking of the Bias Square along the selvage and place the ruler's edge against it. Make the first cut.

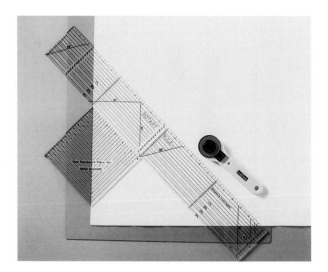

2. Measure the width of the strip from the cut edge of the fabric. Cut along the edge of the ruler.

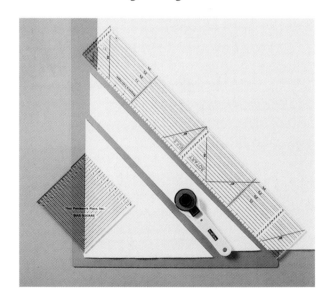

When cutting bias strips, a 24"-long ruler may be too short for several of the cuts. After making several cuts, carefully fold the fabric over itself so that the bias edges are even. Continue to cut bias strips.

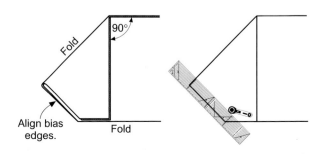

STRIP PIECING

Many of the quilts in this book contain simple units based on four-patch or ninepatch units. Strip piecing is a quick and easy way to mass-produce these units. It eliminates the long and tedious repetition of sewing together individual pieces.

To make four-patch or ninepatch units, first cut strips across the crosswise grain of fabric as shown on page 19.

To determine the width to cut strips, add a $1/4$"-wide seam allowance to each side of the finished dimension on the desired shape. For example, if the finished dimension of a square will be 2", cut $2^1/2$"-wide strips. Strip widths given for all quilts include $1/4$"-wide seam allowances on each side.

Four-Patch Units

1. Sew light and dark strips of fabric together with $1/4$"-wide seam allowances.
2. Press seam allowances toward the darker fabric, pressing from the right side so the fabric won't pleat along the seam lines. Usually, pressing toward the dark fabric will result in opposing seams.
3. Place these two sewn strips together, with right sides facing, reversing the colors as shown. The seam allowances will face opposite directions.

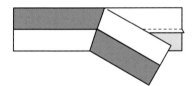

4. Cut sewn strips in pairs, beginning at the left side of the strip and working toward the right. The width of the cut is specified in the directions for each quilt.

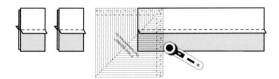

5. Stitch pairs together with $1/4$"-wide seams to complete a Four Patch block. (See page 30 for chain-piecing details.)

6. Press seam to one side.

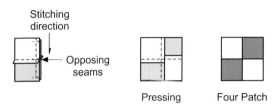

Stitching direction

Opposing seams

Pressing   Four Patch

Ninepatch Units

Ninepatches are made using the same principle but with three strips of fabric. You need to make two different strip sets.

1. To make Strip Set 1, sew one light strip between two dark strips, using $1/4$"-wide seams. Press seams toward the dark fabric.

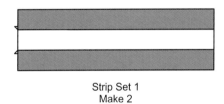

Strip Set 1
Make 2

2. To make Strip Set 2, sew one dark strip between two light strips, using $1/4$"-wide seams. Press seams toward the dark fabric.

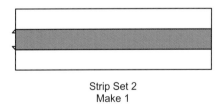

Strip Set 2
Make 1

3. Place a Strip Set 1 and a Strip Set 2 together, with right sides facing. The seam allowances will face opposite directions.

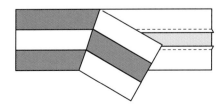

4. Cut strip sets in pairs. Begin at the left side of the strip and work toward the right. The width of the cut is specified in the directions for each quilt.

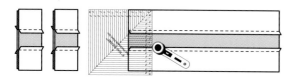

5. Stitch pairs together with ¼"-wide seams. (See page 30 for chain-piecing directions.)

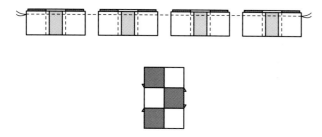

6. Cut the remaining Strip Set 1 into pieces the same width as the pieces you cut for the pairs.

7. Stitch the remaining pieces to the previously sewn pairs to complete the Ninepatch blocks.

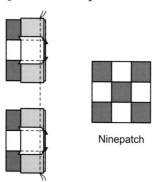

Ninepatch

8. Press seams as shown.

TIP: If you want strip-pieced units to contain a variety of fabrics instead of identical fabric combinations, vary the strips in the strip sets. Select a different combination of fabrics for each strip set and change the positions of the fabrics within the strip sets.

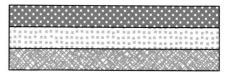

Strip Set 1

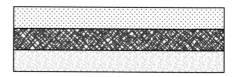

Strip Set 2

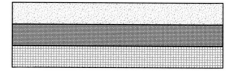

Strip Set 3

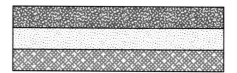

Strip Set 4

Your completed blocks will have variety of scrappy fabric combinations.

BASIC BIAS SQUARE TECHNIQUE

Many traditional quilt patterns contain squares made from two contrasting half-square triangles. The short sides of the triangles are on the straight grain of fabric while the long sides are on the bias. These are called bias-square units. Using a bias strip-piecing method, you can easily sew and cut large amounts of bias squares. This technique is especially useful for small bias squares, where pressing after stitching usually distorts the shape (and sometimes burns fingers).

NOTE: All directions in this book give the cut size for bias squares; the finished size after stitching will be 1/2" smaller.

You will need to cut a sizable amount of bias squares for most of the quilts in this book. Use the technique shown below to help conserve time and fabric. Cut strips from fat quarters (18" x 22") or fat eighths (9" x 22") of fabric. The directions specify the fabrics to use and the width of the strips to cut.

1. Layer two pieces of fabric, *right sides facing up*, and cut as shown. Starting at the corner of the fabric, make the first cut at a 45° angle.

18"

Layer fabrics with right sides up.

Begin first cut at the corner.

2. Arrange the strips in the order you will sew them. Beginning with the triangular piece in either corner, select a strip from the top layer. Then select the strip next to it from the bottom layer. Continue to select strips in this manner, alternating from the top and bottom layers as you move toward the opposite corner of the strips. This will give you two sets of strips to sew together.

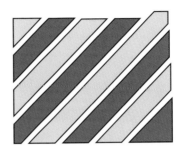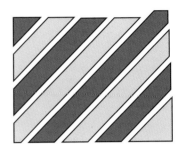

3. Sew the strips together along the long bias edge, right sides facing, with 1/4"-wide seams. Offset the edges 1/4" as shown.

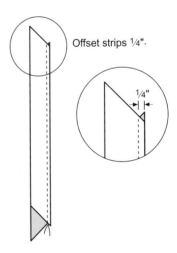

Offset strips 1/4".

1/4"

Fat Quarters Cutting Chart for Bias Squares

Based on 1 light and 1 dark fat quarter (18" x 22") of fabric.

Strip Width	Cut Size of Bias Square	Yield	Finished Size of Bias Square
1³/₄"*	1¹/₂"	160	1"
2"*	1³/₄"	120	1¹/₄"
2"	2"	100	1¹/₂"
2¹/₄"	2¹/₄"	80	1³/₄"
2¹/₂"	2¹/₂"	60	2"
2³/₄"	3"	50	2¹/₂"
3"	3¹/₂"	38	3"
3³/₄"	4¹/₂"	24	4"

*Press seams open rather than toward dark fabric.

The lower edge of the pieced rectangle and the adjacent side edge must form a straight line after sewing. The other two edges will be irregular. *It is important to sew in this configuration if strip-pieced fabric is to yield the amount of bias squares indicated by the chart.* Press seams toward the darker fabric. (If cutting bias squares 1¼" or smaller, try pressing the seams open to evenly distribute fabric bulk.)

The illustrations below show the strip-pieced fabric shapes that result when strips are stitched for the most common sizes.

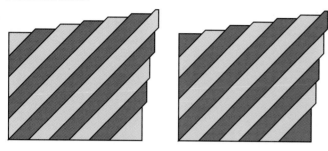

Strip-pieced fabric for 2½" cut (2" finished) bias squares

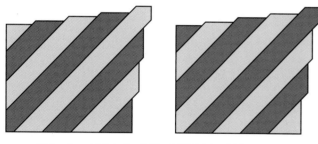

Strip-pieced fabric for 3½" cut (3" finished) bias squares

4. Begin cutting at the left side on the lower edge of each unit. Align the 45° mark of the Bias Square ruler on the seam line. Each bias square will require two cuts. The first cut is along the side and top edge. It removes the bias square from the rest of the fabric and is made slightly larger than the correct size, as shown in the series of illustrations below.

5. The second cut is made along the remaining two sides. It aligns the diagonal and trims the bias square to the correct size

    To make the cut, turn the segment and place the Bias Square on the opposite two sides, aligning the required measurements on both sides of the cutting guide and the 45° mark on the seam. Cut the remaining two sides of the bias squares.

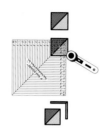

Turn cut segments and cut opposite two sides.

6. Continue cutting bias squares from each unit in this manner, working from left to right and from bottom to top, row by row, until you have cut bias squares from all usable fabric. The chart on page 25 specifies how many bias squares you can expect to cut from 2 fat quarters (18" x 22") of fabric.

TIP: Remember, when cutting bias squares, if you don't have enough fabric to cut a 2½" bias square, cut a smaller size, such as 2¼" or 2", for use in another project. If you cut extra, smaller sizes of bias squares to finish off your bias-square strips, they will accumulate in no time, ready to make into a scrappy quilt.

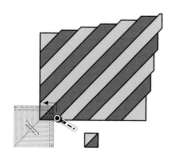 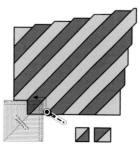 

Align 45° mark on seam line and cut first two sides.

Scrappy Bias Squares

For bias squares with a scrappy look, use a variety of fabrics when you make them. Layer four fat quarters of fabric in two pairs and cut into bias strips. Consult the cutting specifications for the quilt you are making to determine the strip width.

Mix and match the cut bias strips from the four fabrics to form rectangles and squares. Arrange and sew strips by size, placing the left and lower edges as straight as possible. The remaining edges will be uneven.

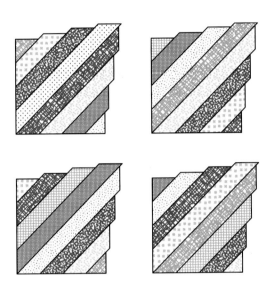

Making Just a Few Bias Squares

If you don't need as many bias squares as a fat quarter yields, but you need more than one or two, start with small squares of fabric. Refer to the chart at right for common sizes and yields.

1. To make just a few bias squares, start with 2 small squares of fabric. Layer with right sides facing up and cut in half diagonally.

2. Cut into strips, measuring from the previous cut.

3. Stitch the strips together using 1/4"-wide seams. Be sure to align the strips so the lower edge and one adjacent edge form straight lines.

4. Starting at the lower left corner, cut bias squares following the directions on page 25.

Use the chart below to determine strip width and resulting yield.

Finished Size	Cut Size	Fabric Size	Strip Width	Yield
2"	2½" x 2½"	8" x 8"*	2½"	8
2"	2½" x 2½"	9" x 9"	2½"	14
2½"	3" x 3"	8" x 8"	2¾"	8
3"	3½" x 3½"	9" x 9"	3"	8

A pair of 7" x 7" squares will yield the same number of bias squares.

It's important to be comfortable with the sewing machine you are using. If this is your first machine-made quilt, practice guiding fabric through the machine. If you leave the machine unthreaded, you can practice over and over on the same pieces of fabric.

Operating a sewing machine requires the same type of coordination it takes to drive a car. You use your foot to control the machine's speed and your hands to control the fabric's direction. To start, use your right foot for the foot pedal to manage the speed. If the machine goes too fast at first, slip a sponge under a hinge-type pedal to slow it down. Use your hands to guide the fabric that feeds into the machine.

A good habit to develop is to use a seam ripper or long pin to gently guide the fabric up to the needle. You can hold seam intersections together or make minor adjustments before the fabric is sewn.

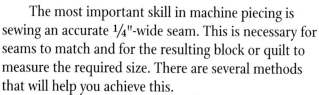

The most important skill in machine piecing is sewing an accurate ¼"-wide seam. This is necessary for seams to match and for the resulting block or quilt to measure the required size. There are several methods that will help you achieve this.

- Purchase a special foot that is sized so that you can align the edge of your fabric with the edge of the presser foot, resulting in a seam that is ¼" away from the fabric edge. Bernina® has a special patch-work foot (#37) and Little Foot makes several special ¼" feet that fit most machines.
- If you have an electronic or computerized sewing machine, adjust the needle position so that the resulting seam is ¼" away from the fabric edge.
- Find the ¼" seam allowance on your machine by placing an accurate template under the presser foot and lowering the needle onto the seam line; mark the seam allowance by placing a piece of masking tape at the edge of the template. You can use several layers of masking tape, building up a raised edge to guide your fabric. You can also use a piece of moleskin for a raised seam guide. Test to make sure that the

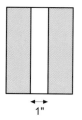

Template | Tape

¼"

method you are using results in an accurate ¼"-wide seam.

1. Cut three strips of fabric, each 1½" x 3".
2. Sew the strips together, using the edge of the presser foot or the seam guide you have made.
3. Press seams toward the outer edges. After sewing and pressing, the center strip should measure exactly 1" wide. If it doesn't, adjust the needle or seam guide in the proper direction.

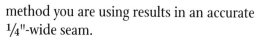

1"

MATCHING SEAMS

When sewing the fabric pieces that make up a unit or block, follow the piecing diagram provided. Press each group of pieces before joining it to the next unit.

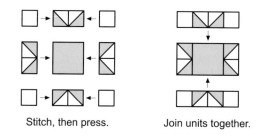

Stitch, then press.   Join units together.

There are several techniques you can use to get your seams to match perfectly.

OPPOSING SEAMS: When stitching one seamed unit to another, press seams that need to match in opposite directions. The two "opposing" seams will hold each other in place and evenly distribute the fabric bulk. Plan pressing to take advantage of opposing seams. You will find this particularly important in strip piecing.

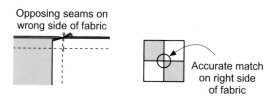

Opposing seams on wrong side of fabric

Accurate match on right side of fabric

POSITIONING PIN: A pin, carefully pushed straight through two points that need to match and pulled tight, will establish the proper matching point. Pin the remainder of the seam normally and remove the positioning pin just before stitching.

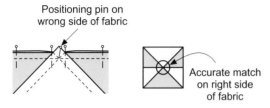

THE X: When triangles are pieced, the stitches will form an X at the next seam line. Stitch through the center of the X to make sure the points on the sewn triangles will not be cut off.

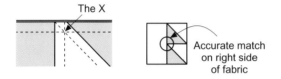

EASING: When two pieces you are sewing together are supposed to match but are slightly different in length, pin the points to match and stitch with the shorter piece on top. The feed dogs will ease the fullness of the bottom piece.

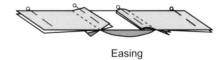

Easing

Inspect each intersection from the right side to see that it is matched. If the seams do not meet accurately, note which direction the fabric needs to be moved. Use a seam ripper to rip out the seam intersection and $1/2$" of stitching on either side of the intersection. Shift fabric to correct the alignment, place positioning pins, then restitch.

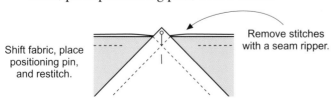

Shift fabric, place positioning pin, and restitch.

Remove stitches with a seam ripper.

PRESSING: After stitching a seam, it is important to press your work. Careful pressing helps make the next steps in the stitching process, such as matching points or aligning seams, easier.

Be sure to *press*, not *iron*, your work. Ironing is an aggressive back-and-forth motion that we use on clothing to remove wrinkles. This action can easily pull and distort the bias edges or seams in your piecing. Perfectly marked and sewn quilt pieces are commonly distorted by excessive ironing. You may notice this particularly after sewing what were two perfectly marked, cut, and sewn triangles into a square. Many times the finished unit is no longer square after you've ironed it. Pressing is the gentle lowering, pressing, and lifting of the iron along the length of the fabric without moving the iron back and forth along the seam. Let the heat, steam, and an occasional spritz of water press the fabric in the desired direction.

MATCHING BLOCKS

Rows of blocks should be pinned together at strategic intersections to ensure accurate matching as rows are sewn together. The process is similar to matching seams within a block.

To make this process easier, plan for opposing seams when you press blocks after stitching. Press seams in opposite directions from row to row.

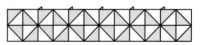

Row 1 — Press seams to right.

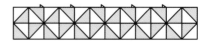

Row 2 — Press seams to left.

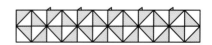

Row 3 — Press seams to right.

The points of carefully matched rows of blocks meet ¼" from the raw edge when rows are sewn together.

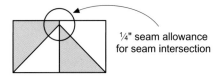

¼" seam allowance for seam intersection

Use positioning pins to hold seam allowances in place. Remove the pins before stitching through the seam intersection.

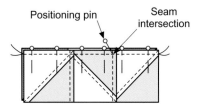

Positioning pin   Seam intersection

CHAIN PIECING

Chain piecing is an assembly-line approach to putting your blocks together. Rather than sewing each block from start to finish, you can sew identical units of each block together at one time, streamlining the process. It's a good idea, however, to sew one sample block together from start to finish to ensure that the pieces have been accurately cut and that you have the proper positioning and coloration for each piece.

Stack the units you will be sewing in pairs, arranging any opposing seam allowances so that the top seam allowance faces toward the needle and the lower seam allowance faces toward you. Then you won't need to keep checking to see if the lower seam is being pulled to the wrong side by the feed dogs as you feed the fabric through the sewing machine.

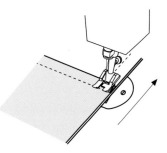

Face top seam allowance toward the needle whenever possible.

Feed units through the machine without stopping to cut thread. There will be a "stitch" or small length of thread between the units.

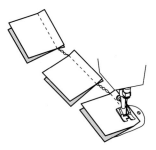

Take the connected units to the ironing board for pressing, then clip them apart. Chain piecing takes a little planning, but it saves you time and thread.

Use a thread saver to begin and end all your seams. Keep a stack of fabric scraps, about 2" x 2", near your machine. When you begin to sew, fold one of the squares in half and sew to its edge. Leave the presser foot down and continue sewing onto your piecing unit. When you have finished sewing a seam or chain piecing, sew onto another thread saver, leaving the needle in place and the presser foot down. This thread saver will be in place for sewing the next seam or unit.

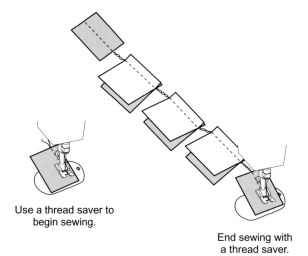

Use a thread saver to begin sewing.

End sewing with a thread saver.

This technique saves thread because you don't stop and pull a length of thread to remove fabric from the machine. All the tails of thread will be on the thread saver and not on the back of the block or quilt. This method also keeps the machine from eating the edges of the fabric as you start a seam.

Appliqué

Some of the quilts in this book have appliquéd accents. Use the paper-patch technique that follows.

1. Make a stiffened template of each shape in the appliqué design. Do not add seam allowances to the templates.
2. On bond-weight paper or freezer paper, trace around the stiffened templates to make a paper patch for each shape in the appliqué.
3. Pin or iron each paper patch to the wrong side of the fabric. If using freezer paper, pin with the plastic-coated side facing out.

4. Cut out the fabric shapes, adding a 1/4"-wide seam allowance around each paper shape.
5. With your fingers, turn the seam allowance over the edge of the paper and baste to the paper. Clip corners and do inside curves first. (A little clipping may be necessary to help the fabric stretch.) On outside curves, take small running stitches through the fabric, only to ease in fullness.
6. For sharply pointed corners, such as the steeple roof in the "Old Country Church" pattern, first fold the corner to the inside. Then fold the remaining seam allowances over the paper.

| Fold corners to inside. | Fold lower edge over paper. | Fold remaining seam allowances over paper. |

Take an occasional stitch through the paper to hold the fabric in place. Follow this basting order (inside curves first, outside curves last) when appliquéing the fabric piece to the block, easing fullness and bias stretch outward. When all the seam allowances are turned and basted, press the appliqué pieces. Then position and pin the pieces in place on the background fabric.

1. Use a small blind-hemming stitch and a single strand of matching thread (for example, pink thread for a pink heart) to appliqué shapes to the background fabric.
2. Start the first stitch from the back of the block. Bring the needle up through the background fabric and through the folded edge of the appliqué piece.

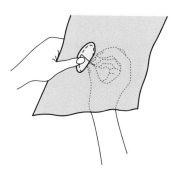

3. Insert the needle right next to where you brought it up, but this time put it through only the background fabric.
4. Bring the needle up through the background fabric and then into the appliqué piece, approximately 1/8" or less from the first stitch.
5. Space your stitches a little less than 1/8" apart.
6. When appliqué is complete, slit the background fabric and pull out the paper patch.

Using This Book

This section contains complete instructions for 21 rotary-cut quilts. All the patterns are written for rotary cutting; a few quilts require appliqué or trimming templates.

All measurements include ¼"-wide seam allowances. Read the complete cutting and piecing directions for the quilt you are going to make before you begin. The patterns are graded as to difficulty, so match the pattern to your skill and patience level.

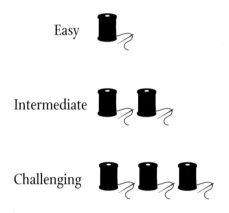

Easy

Intermediate

Challenging

The "Materials" section of each pattern includes fabric and color suggestions. Fabric requirements are based on 44"-wide fabric that has 42 usable inches after washing. If, after preshrinking, your fabric is not at least 42" wide, you may need to purchase more.

Cut strips across the fabric width, selvage to selvage, unless otherwise noted. Cutting specifications are given for strips that are 42" long when cut across the fabric width. If preshrunk fabric is less than 42", you may need to cut an additional strip to cut the required number of pieces.

Many of the quilts specify the purchase of fat quarters and fat eighths. Measure the fat quarters, which should be 18" x 22", and the fat eighths, which should be 9" x 22". You may need to purchase additional fabric if your pieces are smaller than these measurements. If your fabric doesn't yield enough bias squares, substitute scraps of a look-alike fabric. Directions for making small amounts of bias squares are on page 27.

Always cut the largest pieces first from fat quarters or fat eighths, before cutting the smaller pieces. To achieve a scrappy look, purchase a variety of fat quarters or fat eighths. You will not always use all the fabric, so save it for your next scrappy quilt, or use it in one of the leftover projects on pages 94–101.

Cutting instructions are geared for rotary cutting. Quick-cutting and strip-piecing techniques sometimes yield more pieces than are needed to make a particular block or quilt. Don't worry if you have a few more pieces than you need; save them for another scrap project.

All measurements include ¼"-wide seam allowances. *Do not add seam allowances to the dimensions given in the cutting section.* Cutting specifications for triangles indicate the size of the square from which you will cut the triangles. Directions for half-square triangles instruct you to "cut once diagonally"; instructions for quarter-square triangles specify "cut twice diagonally." If you need a refresher, see pages 21–22.

Use the photos and drawings that accompany the patterns as a reference while assembling your quilt. General instructions for finishing your quilt begin on page 102.

Most of the quilts have borders with straight-cut corners rather than mitered corners. You can cut border strips along the crosswise grain and seam to get the length needed. Unless lengthwise borders are included in a quilt plan's fabric requirements, purchase additional fabric if you want to cut borders along the lengthwise grain. *Cut border pieces longer than the dimensions given, then trim to fit when you know the actual dimensions of the center of the quilt top.* (See "Adding Borders" on page 102.) Bindings are made from narrow double-fold bias strips. (See "Binding the Edges" on pages 107–109.)

Evening Star

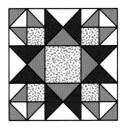

Dimensions: 35" x 44"
Finished Block Size: 9" x 9"

6 blocks, set 2 across and 3 down; 3"-wide inner border and 5½"-wide outer border.

Materials: 44"-wide fabric

6 fat eighths (each 9" x 22") assorted light-background fabrics for blocks.

⅝ yd. light blue for bias squares.

6 rectangles, each 5" x 10", of assorted dark fabrics for blocks.

6 squares, each 5" x 5", of assorted medium fabrics for blocks.

⅞ yd. paisley stripe with 3"-wide motif for inner border (You need 4 complete repeats across the fabric width from selvage to selvage.)

1 yd. large-scale print for outer border

1½ yds. fabric for backing

⅓ yd. fabric for 168" (4¾ yds.) of bias binding

TIPS FOR FABRIC SELECTION: To achieve a scrappy look, use speed-piecing techniques for the bias squares only. Cut the star tips and the remainder of the pieces individually. Mix and match the light fabrics in some of the blocks, matching the center square to the 4 small squares. Use a different light-background fabric for the bias squares and the large triangles along the outside edge.

Cutting

From EACH fat eighth of light fabric, cut:
   1 square, 9" x 9", for bias squares.
   1 square, 3½" x 3½", for block center, for a total of 6 squares.
   1 square, 4¼" x 4¼". Cut the square twice diagonally to make 4 triangles, for a total of 24 triangles (Triangle B).
   4 squares, each 2" x 2", for a total of 24 squares (Square A).
From light blue fabric, cut:
   6 squares, each 9" x 9", for bias squares.
From EACH 5" x 10" rectangle of dark fabric, cut:
   2 squares, each 4¼" x 4¼". Cut each square twice diagonally to make 8 triangles (Triangle C), for a total of 48 triangles.
From EACH 5" square of medium fabric, cut:
   1 square, 4¼" x 4¼". Cut the square twice diagonally to make 4 triangles (Triangle D), for a total of 24 triangles.
From paisley stripe, cut:
   4 strips, each 3½" x 30", along the lengthwise grain of fabric, centering the motif.
From large-scale print, cut:
   4 strips, each 5¾" wide.

Block Assembly

1. Pair each 9" light square with a 9" light blue square, *right sides up*. Cut and sew together 2"-wide bias strips, following the directions for making just a few bias squares on page 27. Cut 12 bias squares, each 2" x 2", from each fabric combination to make 72 bias squares.

2. Arrange and sew together 3 matching bias squares and a background Square A to make corner units.

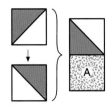

Make 4

3. Join the large triangles to make each side unit.

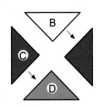

Make 4

4. Join 4 bias-square units, 4 side units, and a light center square to make each Evening Star block.

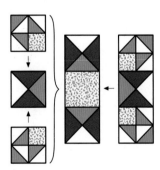 

Make 6

Quilt Top Assembly

1. Join the blocks into 3 rows of 2 blocks each. Sew the rows together.

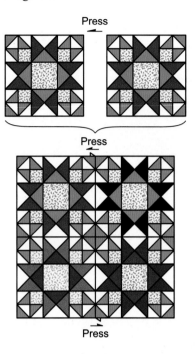

Press

2. Add 3½"-wide paisley strips for the inner border, and 5¾"-wide large-scale print strips for the outer border, following the directions for borders with straight-cut corners on page 102.

Finishing

1. Layer the quilt top with batting and backing; baste. Quilt as desired, or follow the quilting suggestion on page 110. (See "Finishing Techniques" on pages 102–109.)
2. Bind the edges with bias strips of fabric.

EVENING IN PARIS, *pieced by Nancy J. Martin, 1994, Woodinville, Washington, 35" x 44".*
Made from wonderful European fabrics purchased at Le Rouvray in Paris,
this star quilt was made to commemorate a romantic evening on the Bateau Mouches.
Quilted by Sue von Jentzen, Granite Falls, Washington. (Collection of That Patchwork Place, Inc.)

Contrary Wife

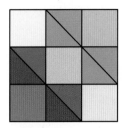

Dimensions: 80" x 80"
Finished Block Size: 7½" x 7½"

64 blocks, set 8 across and 8 down; 10"-wide border.

Materials: 44"-wide fabric

⅜ yd. *each* of 6 beige prints for blocks
⅝ yd. *each* of 6 pink prints for blocks
2½ yds. large-scale floral print for border
6 fat quarters of green prints for blocks
4¾ yds. fabric for backing
⅝ yd. for 330" (9¼ yds.) of bias binding

TIPS FOR FABRIC SELECTION: Choose a large-scale floral print for the border, and let it set the color scheme for this scrappy quilt. If you use an assortment of pink prints in the corners of the Contrary Wife blocks, they will form a diamond shape when the blocks are set together. Form a chain of stars with green triangles and beige squares.

Cutting

From EACH beige print, cut:
  3 strips, each 3" wide. Cut the strips into
    32 squares, each 3" x 3", for a total of 192 beige squares.
From EACH pink print, cut:
  1 fat quarter, 18" x 22", for bias squares.
  4 strips, each 3" x 20". Cut 22 squares, each 3" x 3", for a total of 128 pink squares.
From large-scale floral print, cut along the lengthwise grain:
  2 strips, each 10¼" x 60½", for side borders.
  2 strips, each 10¼" x 80", for top and bottom borders.

Block Assembly

1. Pair the 6 pink and green fat quarters of fabric, placing them right sides up. Cut and sew together 2¾"-wide bias strips, following the directions for making bias squares on pages 25–27. Cut 43 bias squares, each 3" x 3", from each fabric combination (258 total—only 256 are needed).

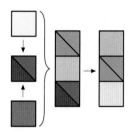

Make 256

2. For each block, arrange 4 bias squares with 3 beige and 2 pink squares. Sew together as shown.

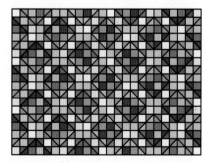

Make 64

Quilt Top Assembly and Finishing

1. Join the blocks into 8 rows of 8 blocks each, arranging colors as shown below and in the photo on page 37. Join the rows to form the quilt top.

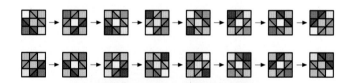

2. Add the 10¼"-wide floral border strips, following the directions for borders with straight-cut corners on page 102.
3. Layer the quilt top with batting and backing; quilt as desired, or follow the quilting suggestion on page 110. (See "Finishing Techniques" on pages 102–109.)
4. Bind the edges with bias strips of fabric.

SWEETNESS AND LIGHT, pieced by Nancy J. Martin, 1994, Woodinville, Washington, 80" x 80".
The sweet color scheme, determined by the paisley print used in the border, suggested an agreeable name
for this quilt made of Contrary Wife blocks.
Quilted by Mrs. Dan R. Miller, Holmes County, Ohio. (Collection of That Patchwork Place, Inc.)

Wonderful World
© Judy Martin

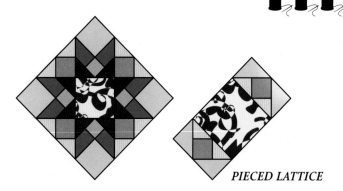

PIECED LATTICE

Dimensions: 67⅞" x 67⅞"
Finished Block Size: 12" x 12"
Finished Pieced Lattice: 6" x 12"

13 blocks, set diagonally with 16 pieced lattices, large sashing squares, and large side setting triangles for sides and corners.

Materials: 44"-wide fabric

2⅞ yds. light blue print for block background, sashing squares, and setting pieces (Fabric A)

⅞ yd. large floral print (Fabric B) for blocks and pieced lattices

⅛ yd. *each* of 4 red prints (Fabric C) for blocks

¼ yd. light green print (Fabric D) for blocks

¼ yd. *each* of 4 dark green prints (Fabric E) for blocks

¼ yd. *each* of 4 medium blue prints (Fabric F) for blocks and pieced lattice

¾ yd. light pink print (Fabric G) for blocks

4¼ yds. fabric for backing

⅝ yd. for 282" (7⅞ yds.) of bias binding

TIPS FOR FABRIC SELECTION: Choose a large-scale floral print for the centers of the blocks and the pieced lattice. Select individual colors from the print for the remaining fabrics. Look for a background fabric with a design that still flows freely after cutting and piecing. Use the following illustrations to aid in fabric placement.

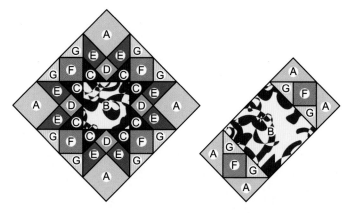

Letters indicate fabric placement.

Cutting

From light blue print (Fabric A), cut:

4 strips, each 3⅞" wide. Cut the strips into 32 squares, each 3⅞" x 3⅞". Cut each square once diagonally to make 64 triangles for lattices.

5 strips, each 3½" wide. Cut the strips into 52 squares, each 3½" x 3½", for blocks.

2 squares, each 27" x 27". Cut each square twice diagonally to make 8 side setting pieces.

2 squares, each 9½" x 9½". Cut each square once diagonally to make 4 corner setting pieces.

4 squares, each 6½" x 6½", for lattice squares.

From large floral print (Fabric B), cut:

16 squares, each 6½" x 6½".

13 squares, each 4¾" x 4¾".

From EACH red print (Fabric C), cut:

1 strip, 3" wide. Cut the strip into 13 squares, each 3" x 3". Cut each square once diagonally for a total of 104 triangles.

From light green print (Fabric D), cut:

3 strips, each 2" wide. Cut the strips into 52 squares, each 2" x 2".

This block is from Judy Martin's book Scraps, Blocks and Quilts ©1990. *Used with permission.*

(Cutting instructions continued on page 40.)

*WONDERFUL WORLD, pieced by Nancy J. Martin, 1994, Woodinville, Washington, 67⅞" x 67⅞".
This has been a favorite pattern of Nancy's ever since she was asked to piece
a version of it for Judy Martin's book* Scraps, Blocks, and Quilts.
Quilted by Hazel Montague, Bellingham, Washington. (Collection of That Patchwork Place, Inc.)

From EACH dark green print (Fabric E), cut:
> 14 Template 1 and 14 Template 1 reversed. (Use Template 1 on page 41). You need a total of 52 pieces and 52 reversed pieces.

From EACH medium blue print (Fabric F), cut:
> 2 strips, each $2^5/8$" wide. Cut the strips into 21 squares, each $2^5/8$" x $2^5/8$", for a total of 84 squares.

From light pink print (Fabric G), cut:
> 5 strips, each $4^1/4$" wide. Cut the strips into 42 squares, each $4^1/4$" x $4^1/4$". Cut each square twice diagonally for a total of 168 triangles.

Block Assembly

1. Make corner units for each block, arranging the pieces and sewing them together as shown.

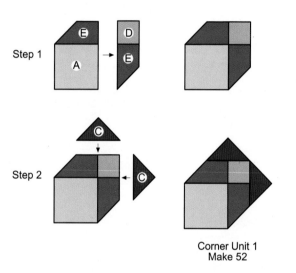

Corner Unit 1
Make 52

2. Sew a corner unit to opposite sides of a $4^3/4$" square cut from Fabric B. Make a total of 13 center units in this manner. Set the remaining corner units aside.

Center Unit
Make 13

3. Arrange 2 triangles (Fabric G) and 1 square (Fabric F) and sew together as shown. Make 32 for the lattice strips and 52 for the blocks.

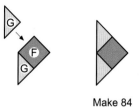

Make 84

4. Sew 2 of the units made in step 3 to each side of the remaining corner units.

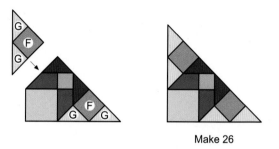

Make 26

5. Sew 2 of the units made in Step 4 to opposite sides of each of the 13 center units to complete blocks.

Make 13

6. For the pieced lattice, join 2 Fabric A triangles to each of 32 of the units made in Step 3. Stitch these units to each 6½" square of Fabric B.

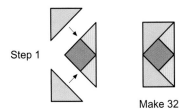

Step 1

Make 32

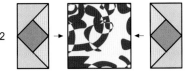

Step 2

Make 16

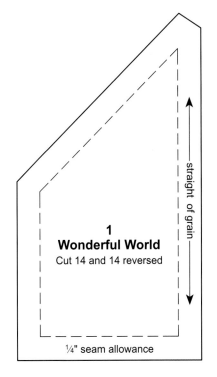

1
Wonderful World
Cut 14 and 14 reversed

straight of grain

¼" seam allowance

Quilt Top Assembly and Finishing

1. Arrange the Wonderful World blocks, pieced lattices, Fabric A lattice squares, and side setting triangles to form the quilt top. Join the pieces in diagonal rows. Sew the rows together to complete the quilt top, adding the corner setting triangles last. Trim excess fabric around the outer edges to leave ¼" of fabric beyond the block corners.

2. Layer the quilt top with batting and backing; baste. Quilt as desired, or follow the quilting suggestion on page 110. (See "Finishing Techniques" on pages 102–109.)

3. Bind the edges with bias strips of fabric.

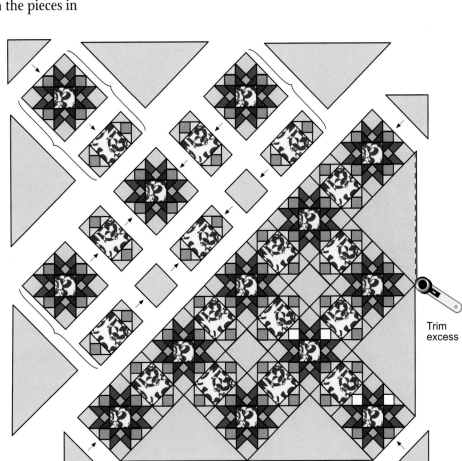

Trim excess

Road to Oklahoma

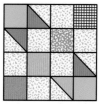
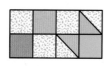

HALF BLOCK B

CORNER BLOCK C

HALF BLOCK A

Dimensions: 60" x 80"
Finished Block Size: 10" x 10"

24 blocks, set 4 across and 6 down, with 20 half blocks and 4 corner blocks; 5"-wide border.

Materials: 44"-wide fabric

2½ yds. light-background fabric for blocks
⅜ yd. *each* of 6 blue prints for blocks
¼ yd. *each* of 3 pink prints for blocks
¼ yd. *each* of 3 lavender prints for blocks
Small yellow scraps (optional) for single star
1¼ yds. blue for border
5½ yds. fabric for backing
⅝ yd. fabric for 290" (8⅛ yds.) of bias binding
Batting and thread to finish

TIPS FOR FABRIC SELECTION: Use 1930s reproduction fabrics to make the stars and chains that form the quilt top. Use blue fabrics for the star pieces, and pink and lavender fabrics for the chains that run diagonally in both directions across the quilt. Choose a special fabric for the single yellow star in the lower corner of the quilt.

Cutting

From light-background print, cut:
6 rectangles, each 12" x 16", for bias squares.
12 strips, each 3" wide. Reserve for four-patch units.
6 strips, each 3" wide. Cut the strips into 72 squares, each 3" x 3".
From EACH blue print, cut:
1 rectangle, 12" x 16", for bias squares (6 total).
12 squares, each 3" x 3" (72 total).
From EACH pink and EACH lavender print, cut:
2 strips, each 3" wide (6 pink and 6 lavender, total); reserve for four-patch units.
From blue fabric for border, cut:
8 strips, each 5¼" wide, for borders.

Block Assembly

1. Pair each 12" x 16" background rectangle with a 12" x 16" blue print rectangle, right sides up. Cut and sew together 2¾"-wide bias strips, following the directions for making bias squares on pages 25–27. Cut 24 bias squares, each 3" x 3", from each fabric combination for a total of 144 bias squares.

Make 144

2. Stitch each 3"-wide pink strip, and each 3"-wide lavender strip to a 3"-wide background strip. Layer and cut into 136 four-patch segments. Sew random pairs of segments together to make 68 four-patch units. See "Four-Patch Units" on page 23.

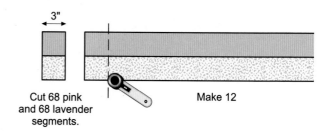

Cut 68 pink and 68 lavender segments.

Make 12

Make 68

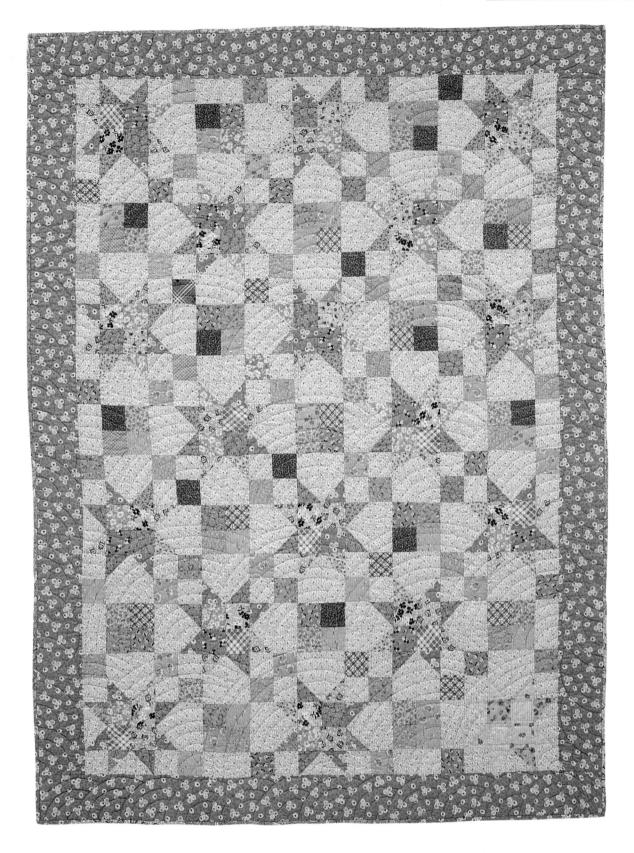

*POT OF GOLD, pieced by Nancy J. Martin, 1994, Woodinville, Washington, 60" x 80".
In past times, the road to Oklahoma was full of adventure seekers looking for the pot of gold
at the end of the rainbow. Hence the choice of Road to Oklahoma quilt blocks, a rainbow
quilting design, and one yellow star to represent the pot of gold. Quilted by Clara Hershberger,
Holmes County, Ohio. (Collection of That Patchwork Place, Inc.)*

3. For each Road to Oklahoma block, arrange and sew together 4 bias squares, 2 four-patch units, 2 background squares, and 2 blue squares.

NOTE: Place the four-patch segments randomly in each block.

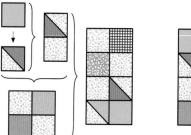
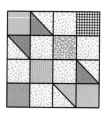

Make 24

4. For each half Block A and B, arrange and sew 2 bias squares, 1 four-patch unit, 1 background square, and 1 blue square, following the illustration below.

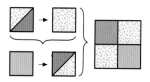
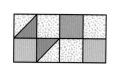

Half Block A
Make 10

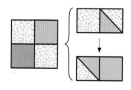
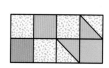

Half Block B
Make 10

5. For each corner Block C, arrange and sew 2 bias squares, 1 background square, and 1 blue square.

Corner Block C
Make 4

6. Arrange blocks, half blocks, and corner blocks on a design wall. Turn the blocks so that blue stars are formed and there is a diagonal chain of the pink and lavender squares in both directions. Use half blocks and corner blocks to complete the design.

7. Add the 5¼"-wide blue border strips, following the directions for borders with straight-cut corners on page 102.
8. Layer the quilt top with batting and backing; baste. Quilt as desired, or follow the quilting suggestion on page 110. (See "Finishing Techniques" on pages 102–109.)
9. Bind the edges with bias strips of fabric.

Ribbon Block

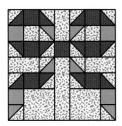

Dimensions: 57" x 57"
Finished Block Size: 14" x 14"

5 blocks (4 pieced, 1 appliquéd), set diagonally with large side setting triangles; 1½"-wide inner border, 4½"-wide pieced-ribbon middle border, 3"-wide outer border.

Materials: 44"-wide fabric

3¾ yds. light-background print for blocks, side setting triangles, and inner, pieced, and outer borders
⅞ yd. light pink for pieced bows, border, and heart appliqué
1⅛ yd. dark pink for pieced bows and border
3⅞ yds. fabric for backing
½ yd. fabric for 238" (6⅝ yds.) of bias binding
Optional:
    18" x 18" lace doily
    Assorted buttons for embellishment
    2 yds. ¼"-wide pink ribbon for heart

TIPS FOR FABRIC SELECTION: Select light and dark pink fabrics for the Ribbon block and pieced border. The lace doily, sewn to the top after the blocks have been set together, and the button and ribbon embellishment are optional. A single heart appliqué or a four-heart appliqué design can be used in the center. (Use the templates on page 49.)

Cutting

NOTE: Cut all borders along the lengthwise grain.

From light-background print, cut:
    2 strips, each 2" x 40," for inner side borders.
    2 strips, each 2" x 43", for inner top and bottom borders.
    2 strips, each 3¼" x 52", for outer side borders.
    2 strips, each 3¼" x 57½", for outer top and bottom borders.
    1 square, 21¼" x 21¼". Cut twice diagonally for 4 side setting triangles.
    2 squares, each 10⅞" x 10⅞". Cut each once diagonally for 4 corner setting triangles.
    3 fat quarters, each 18" x 22", for bias squares (A and B).
    1 square, 14½" x 14½", for background of appliqué block.
    8 squares, each 4½" x 4½", for Ribbon blocks (Square G).
    12 rectangles, each 2½" x 4½", for Ribbon blocks (Rectangle F).
    8 squares, each 2½" x 2½", for Ribbon blocks (Square C).
    4 rectangles, each 2½" x 8½", for Ribbon blocks (Rectangle H).
    8 squares, each 4⅛" x 4⅛". Cut each square twice diagonally to make 32 small triangles for pieced border.
    7 squares, each 7" x 7". Cut each square twice diagonally to make 28 large triangles for pieced border.
    2 squares, each 6¾" x 6¾". Cut each square once diagonally to make 4 triangles for pieced border corners.
From light pink fabric, cut:
    1 fat quarter, 18" x 22", for bias squares (B).
    3 strips, each 2½" wide. Cut the strips into 48 squares, each 2½" x 2½" (Square E). Use 16 squares for Ribbon blocks and reserve 32 squares for pieced border.
    1 heart for appliqué, using Large Heart Template 2 on page 49;
    OR
    4 hearts for appliqué, using Small Heart Template 3 on page 49.

From dark pink fabric, cut:

2 fat quarters, each 18" x 22", for bias squares (A).

4 strips, each 2$\frac{1}{2}$" wide. Cut the strips into 60 squares, each 2$\frac{1}{2}$" x 2$\frac{1}{2}$" (Square D). Use 28 squares for Ribbon blocks and reserve 32 squares for pieced ribbon border.

1 strip, 4$\frac{1}{8}$" wide. Cut the strip into 7 squares, each 4$\frac{1}{8}$" x 4$\frac{1}{8}$". Cut each square twice diagonally to make 28 small triangles for pieced ribbon border.

Block Assembly

1. To make the light pink bias squares (B), pair the light-background print and light pink fat quarters *with right sides up.* Cut and sew together 2$\frac{1}{2}$"-wide bias strips. (See directions for making bias squares on pages 25–27.) Cut 24 bias squares, each 2$\frac{1}{2}$" x 2$\frac{1}{2}$". Save leftovers for another project.

2$\frac{1}{2}$"

Light pink bias
squares (B)
Cut 24

2. To make the dark pink bias squares (A), pair the 2 remaining light-background print and the dark pink fat quarters *with right sides up.* Cut and sew together 2$\frac{1}{2}$"-wide bias strips. Cut 80 bias squares, each 2$\frac{1}{2}$" x 2$\frac{1}{2}$". Use 48 bias squares for the Ribbon blocks and reserve 32 squares for the pieced ribbon border. Save leftovers for another quilt project.

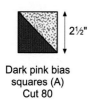

2$\frac{1}{2}$"

Dark pink bias
squares (A)
Cut 80

3. Arrange the bias squares and cut pieces, following the piecing illustration. Sew the pieces into units as shown; join the units to make 4 Ribbon blocks.

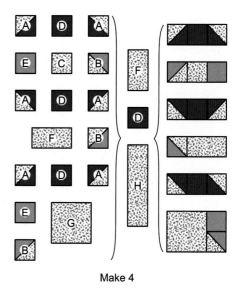

Make 4

4. If you are not using the lace doily, appliqué a single heart or 4 smaller hearts to the center of the background square. Use the heart templates on page 49 and refer to the illustration on page 45 for placement. (See "Appliqué" on page 31.)

Quilt Top Assembly

1. Join Ribbon blocks, center block (with or without appliqué), side setting triangles, then corner triangles to form the quilt top.

BUTTONS AND BOWS, pieced by Nancy J. Martin, 1994, Woodinville, Washington, 57" x 57".
Diagonally set ribbon blocks surround a lace doily embellished with an appliqué heart, buttons, and bows.
A pieced ribbon border surrounds this delightfully romantic quilt.
Quilted by Sue von Jentzen, Granite Falls, Washington. (Collection of That Patchwork Place, Inc.)

2. If you are using a lace doily at the center, place it over the center section formed by the Ribbon blocks. Stitch it to the quilt top by hand or machine. Appliqué the heart in the center of the doily, anchoring it through all layers.

Borders

1. Add 2"-wide background strips for the inner border, following the directions for borders with straight-cut corners on page 102. After adding the inner borders, make sure the quilt top measures 43" x 43" so that the pieced border will fit. If it does not, adjust inner border widths to make it the correct size.

2. Arrange and sew together dark pink bias squares (A) and cut pieces to make 2 pieced borders.

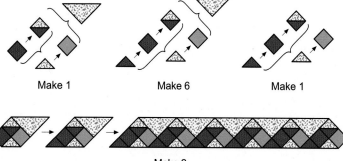

3. Arrange and sew the 2 remaining borders.

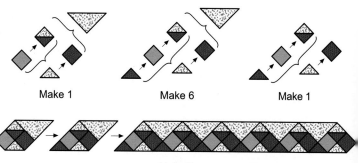

4. Stitch a border to each side of the quilt, matching corner-square colors. Begin and end stitching ¼" from the corners of the quilt and borders, leaving the seam at the corner open.

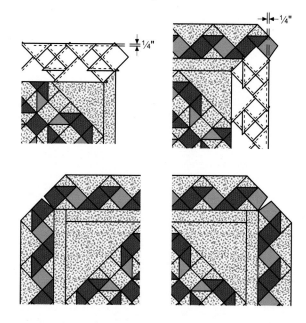

5. Stitch borders together at each corner of quilt.

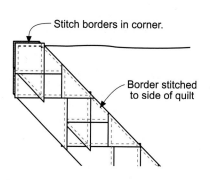

6. Stitch the triangles to the corners of the pieced borders. Trim excess if needed.

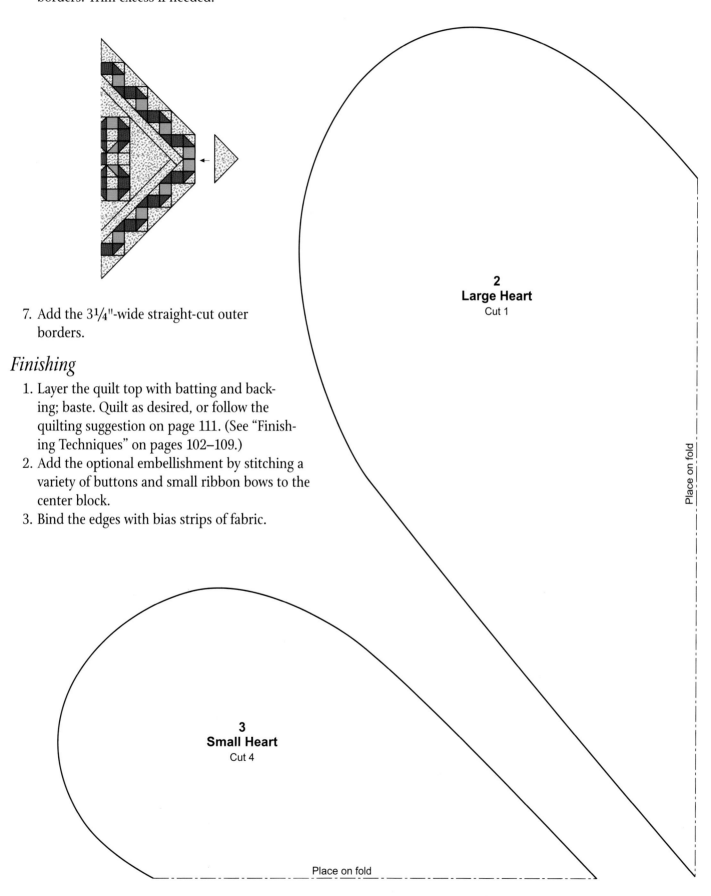

7. Add the 3$\frac{1}{4}$"-wide straight-cut outer borders.

Finishing

1. Layer the quilt top with batting and backing; baste. Quilt as desired, or follow the quilting suggestion on page 111. (See "Finishing Techniques" on pages 102–109.)
2. Add the optional embellishment by stitching a variety of buttons and small ribbon bows to the center block.
3. Bind the edges with bias strips of fabric.

2
Large Heart
Cut 1

Place on fold

3
Small Heart
Cut 4

Place on fold

Old Country Church

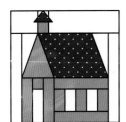

Dimensions: 68$\frac{1}{2}$" x 81"
Finished Block Size: 10" x 10"

20 blocks, set 4 across and 5 down with 2$\frac{1}{2}$"-wide sashing strips; 8"-wide outer border.

Materials: 44"-wide fabric

1$\frac{7}{8}$ yds. muslin for block background
10 fat quarters (18" x 22") of indigo blue prints for blocks
2 yds. light-background print for sashing
2$\frac{1}{8}$ yds. fabric for border (cut along the lengthwise grain)
5 yds. fabric for backing
$\frac{1}{2}$ yd. fabric for 309" (8$\frac{5}{8}$ yds.) of bias binding

TIPS FOR FABRIC SELECTION: Mix and match the indigo blue prints, combining a different roof and church for each block. Use each indigo blue print to make 2 churches and 2 roofs. Use the same fabric for the church and steeple roofs. Select a navy blue print with a light background for the sashing.

Cutting

From muslin, cut:
2 strips, each 1$\frac{1}{2}$" wide. Cut the strips into 20 rectangles, each 1$\frac{1}{2}$" x 3$\frac{1}{2}$", for doors.
3 strips, each 1$\frac{1}{2}$" wide. Cut the strips into 40 rectangles, each 1$\frac{1}{2}$" x 2$\frac{1}{2}$", for windows.
10 strips, each 1$\frac{1}{2}$" wide. Cut the strips into 40 rectangles, each 1$\frac{1}{2}$" x 8$\frac{1}{2}$", for sides of block.
2 strips, each 2$\frac{1}{2}$" wide. Cut the strips into 20 rectangles, each 2$\frac{1}{2}$" x 3", for sky.
4 strips, each 2$\frac{1}{2}$" wide. Cut the strips into 20 rectangles, each 2$\frac{1}{2}$" x 7", for sky.
1 strip, 1$\frac{1}{2}$" wide. Cut the strip into 20 squares, each 1$\frac{1}{2}$" x 1$\frac{1}{2}$", for sky.
3 strips, each 4$\frac{3}{4}$" wide; cut 20 Template 4 and 20 Template 4 reversed for sky, using Template 4 on page 54.

From EACH fat quarter of indigo blue print, cut:
2 peaks for roof, using Template 5 on page 54.
4 rectangles, each 1$\frac{1}{2}$" x 4$\frac{1}{2}$", for sides of door.
4 squares, each 1$\frac{1}{2}$" x 1$\frac{1}{2}$", for top of door and steeple.
6 rectangles, each 1$\frac{1}{2}$" x 2$\frac{1}{2}$", for vertical strips between windows.
4 rectangles, each 1$\frac{1}{2}$" x 5$\frac{1}{2}$", for strips above and below windows.
2 pieces for roof, using Template 6 on page 54.
2 pieces for steeple roof, using Template 7 on page 54. Add seam allowances when you use paper-patch appliqué. (See "Appliqué" on page 31.)

From light-background print, cut:
5 strips, each 3" x 65$\frac{1}{2}$", along the lengthwise grain of fabric, for vertical sashing.
24 strips, each 3" x 10$\frac{1}{2}$", for horizontal sashing.

(Cutting instructions continued on page 52.)

*GOING TO MEETING, pieced by Nancy J. Martin, 1994, Woodinville, Washington, 68¹/₂" x 81".
Old Country Church blocks made from a collection of indigo prints produce a satisfying traditional look.
Architectural details of the churches were emphasized by Alvina Nelson's quilting.
Quilted in Salina, Kansas. (Collection of That Patchwork Place, Inc.)*

From border fabric, cut:
  2 strips, each 8¼" x 65½", along the lengthwise
     grain of fabric, for side borders.
  2 strips, each 8¼" x 68½", along the lengthwise
     grain of fabric, for top and bottom borders.

Block Assembly

1. Arrange and sew pieces 4, 4 reversed, 5 and, 6 to
   make the roof section.

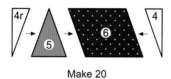

Make 20

2. Arrange and sew the door section.

Make 20

3. Arrange and sew the window section.

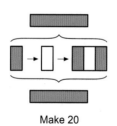

Make 20

4. Join the door and window sections together, add
   the roof section, then add a 1½" x 8½" muslin
   rectangle to each side.

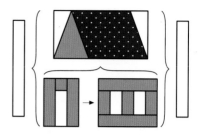

5. Sew the sky portion of the block.

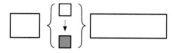

6. Appliqué steeple roof 7 to the top of the steeple,
   using your favorite appliqué method; then sew the
   sky section to the roof section. (See "Appliqué" on
   page 31.)

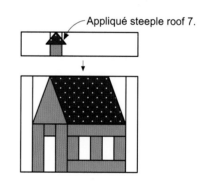

Appliqué steeple roof 7.

Quilt Top Assembly and Finishing

1. Alternate 5 blocks with 6 horizontal sashing strips to make a vertical row. Press the seam allowances toward the sashing strips. Sew a vertical sashing strip between each row and to each side.

2. Add 8¼"-wide border strips, following directions for borders with straight-cut corners on page 102.
3. Layer the quilt top with batting and backing; baste. Quilt as desired, or follow the quilting suggestion on page 111. (See "Finishing Techniques" on pages 102–109.)
4. Bind the edges with bias strips of fabric.

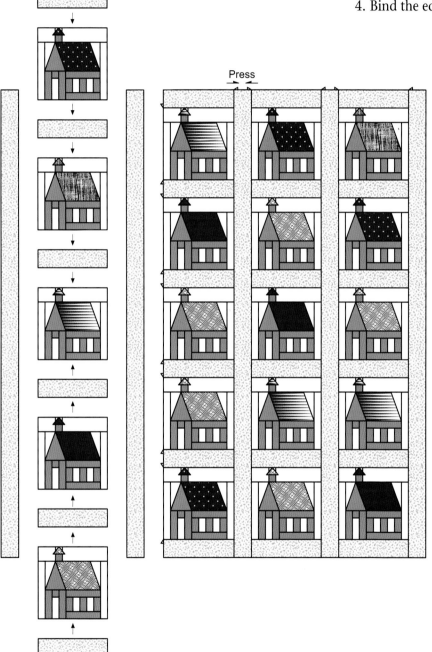

Press

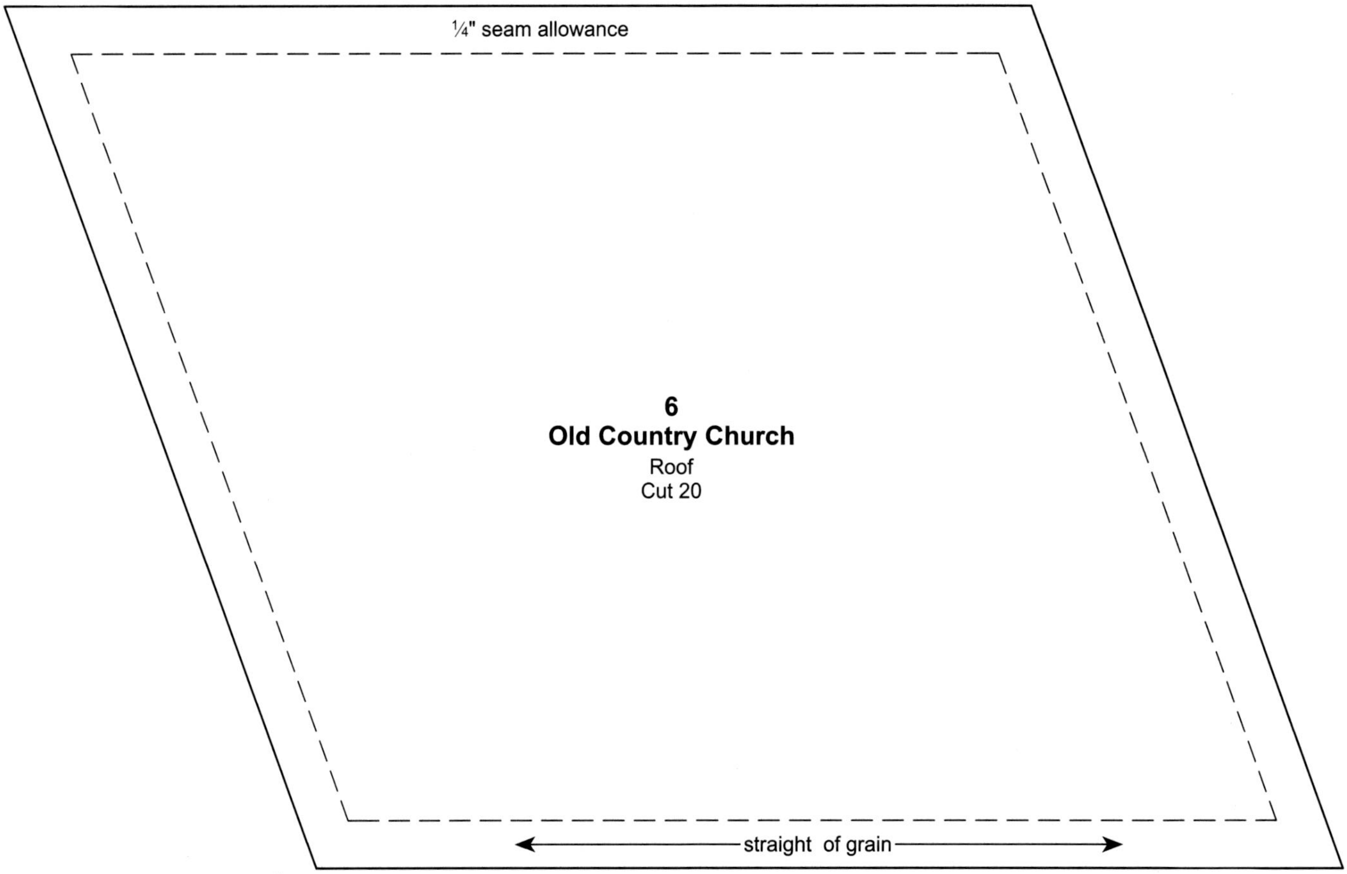

¼" seam allowance

6
Old Country Church
Roof
Cut 20

◄─────── straight of grain ───────►

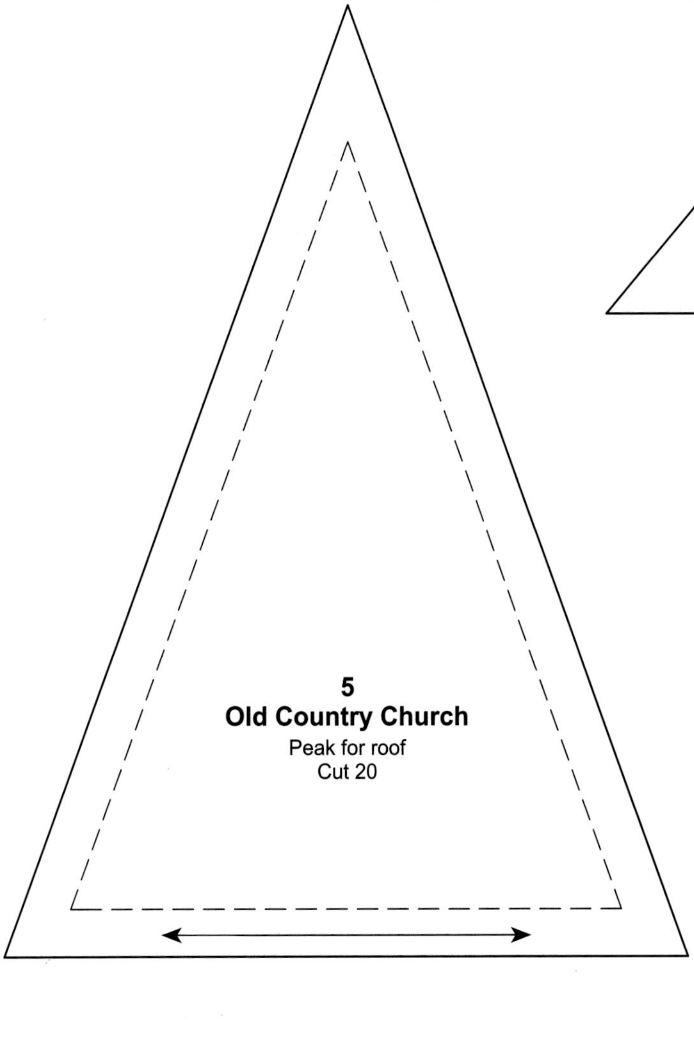

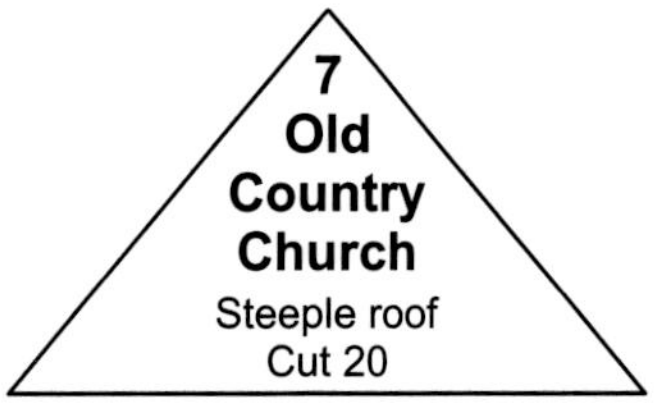

7
Old Country Church
Steeple roof
Cut 20

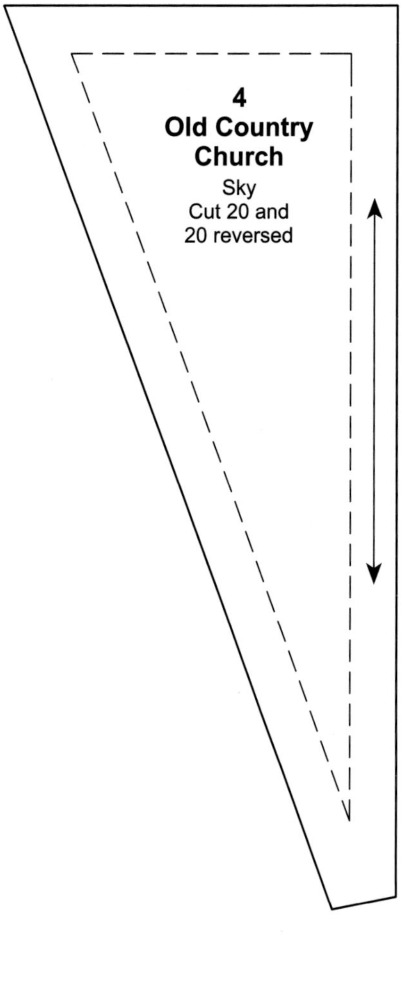

4
Old Country Church
Sky
Cut 20 and
20 reversed

5
Old Country Church
Peak for roof
Cut 20

¼" seam allowance

Goose in the Pond

Dimensions: 60 1/8" x 81 3/8"
Finished Block Size: 10 5/8" x 10 5/8"

18 blocks alternate with 17 plain blocks, set 5 across and 7 down; 1"-wide inner border, 2 1/2"-wide outer border.

Materials: 44"-wide fabric

2 7/8 yds. indigo blue print for block centers, alternate blocks, and border
1 1/2 yds. muslin for blocks
1 1/8 yds. small-scale black-and-white print for blocks
1 1/8 yd. pink-on-pink print for blocks
3 3/4 yds. fabric for backing
1/2 yd. fabric for 293" (8 1/4 yds.) bias binding

TIPS FOR FABRIC SELECTION: Select reproduction fabrics to get the antique appearance of the indigo blue, double pink (or pink-on-pink), and black-and-white small-scale prints. Use muslin for the geese units to emphasize the diagonal design created by the indigo blue alternate blocks.

Cutting

From indigo blue print, cut:
2 strips, each 3 1/2" wide. Cut the strips into 18 squares, each 3 1/2" x 3 1/2".
6 strips, each 11 1/8" wide. Cut the strips into 17 squares, each 11 1/8" x 11 1/8", for alternate blocks.
8 strips, each 2 3/4" wide, for outer border.

From muslin, cut:
6 strips, each 4 1/4" wide. Cut the strips into 54 squares, each 4 1/4" x 4 1/4". Cut each square twice diagonally to make 216 quarter-square triangles.
3 strips, each 3" wide. Cut the strips into 36 squares, each 3" x 3". Cut each square once diagonally to make 72 half-square triangles for block corners.
8 strips, each 1 1/2" wide, for inner border.

From black-and-white print, cut:
13 strips, each 2 3/8" wide. Cut the strips into 216 squares, each 2 3/8" x 2 3/8". Cut each square once diagonally to make 432 triangles.

From pink-on-pink print, cut:
4 strips, each 7 5/8" wide. Cut the strips into 18 squares, each 7 5/8" x 7 5/8". Cut each square twice diagonally to make 72 triangles.

Block Assembly

1. Sew 2 black-and-white triangles to a muslin quarter-square triangle to make a flying geese unit; then sew the units together in groups of 3. Press in the direction of the arrows.

Flying geese unit
Make 216

Press

Make 72

Quilt Top Assembly and Finishing

2. Sew a pink-on-pink triangle to each side of a unit made in step 1. Be sure to orient the geese unit correctly.

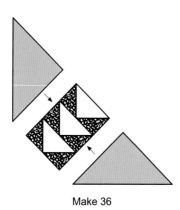

Make 36

3. Sew a unit made in step 1 to opposite sides of an indigo square. Be sure to orient the geese correctly.

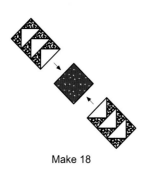

Make 18

4. Sew 2 of the units made in step 2 to opposite sides of a unit made in step 3. Sew a muslin corner triangle to each corner.

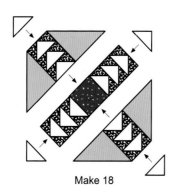

Make 18

1. To make Row A, join 3 blocks to 2 alternate blocks. To make Row B, join 2 blocks to 3 alternate blocks.

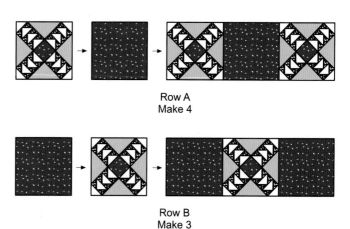

Row A
Make 4

Row B
Make 3

2. Starting with Row A and alternating Rows A and B, sew rows together to form the quilt top.

3. Add the 1½"-wide muslin strips for the inner border and the 2¾"-wide indigo blue strips for the outer border, following the directions for borders with straight-cut corners on page 102.

4. Layer the quilt top with batting and backing; baste. Quilt as desired, or follow the quilting suggestion on page 111. (See "Finishing Techniques" on pages 102–109.)

5. Bind the edges with bias strips of fabric.

MARTHA'S FLYING GEESE, by Carol Dunklau, 1992, Lincoln, Nebraska, 56" x 76".
Carol made this quilt from turn-of-the-century fabrics that had belonged to her husband's grandmother,
Martha Krueger Koehn. Note: The pattern in this book calls for units sized more appropriately for
rotary cutting and produces a 60⅛" x 81⅜" quilt. (Collection of Carol Dunklau.)

Dutchman's Puzzle

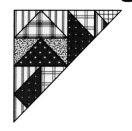

HALF BLOCK

Dimensions: 42½" x 56½"
Finished Block Size: 10" x 10"

11 blocks and 2 half blocks, set diagonally 3 across and 4 down in a strippy setting to create a zigzag effect.

Materials: 44"-wide fabric

8 fat eighths (9" x 22") of assorted light blue-and-tan prints for blocks
8 fat eighths of assorted dark blue-and-tan prints for blocks
1¾ yds. blue print for sashing
2¾ yds. fabric for backing
½ yd. for 208" (5¾ yds.) of bias binding

TIPS FOR FABRIC SELECTION: For this energetic quilt, choose a lively assortment of checks, plaids, stripes, and prints in blue and tan. For each block, use the darker prints for the large triangles and the lighter background prints for the small triangles. Remember that light and dark are relative terms, so some medium prints can be used as either a dark or light fabric, depending upon the fabrics placed next to them. A dark print emphasizes the strippy sashing.

Cutting

From EACH light blue-and-tan print, cut:
13 squares, each 3⅜" x 3⅜". Cut each square once diagonally to make 26 triangles; you need a total of 200.

From EACH dark blue-and-tan print, cut:
3 squares, each 6¼" x 6¼". Cut each square twice diagonally to make 12 triangles. Using one of the triangles as a pattern, cut 4 additional triangles from scraps for a total of 100.

From blue print for sashing, cut:
5 squares, each 15½" x 15½". Cut each square twice diagonally to make 20 side setting pieces.
4 squares, each 8" x 8". Cut each square once diagonally to make 8 corner setting triangles.

Block Assembly

1. Sew 2 light triangles to each dark triangle. Sew 2 of these units together.

Make 8

Make 4

2. Sew 4 units together as shown, rotating each unit to make the Dutchman's Puzzle block.

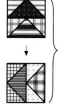

Make 11

3. Use the remaining triangles to piece 2 half blocks as shown. Cut diagonally, trimming away excess and leaving a ¼"-wide seam allowance.

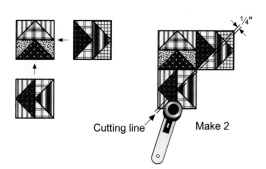

Cutting line   Make 2

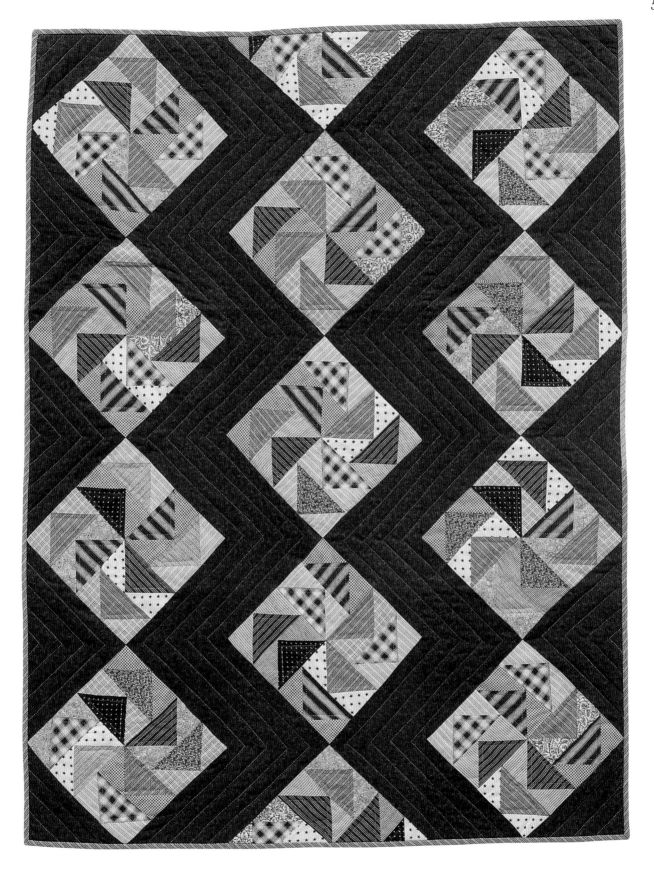

DUTCHMAN'S PUZZLE, *pieced by Nancy J. Martin, 1994, Woodinville, Washington, 42½" x 56½".*
A collection of woven plaids and stripes, purchased from a shop in Belgium, lend character to this lively design.
Quilted by Donna K. Gundlach, Olympia, Washington. (Collection of That Patchwork Place, Inc.)

Quilt Top Assembly and Finishing

1. Arrange and sew 4 blocks, 4 corner setting triangles, and 6 side setting triangles into a row. Press the seam allowances toward the setting triangles.

Outer rows
Make 2

2. Arrange and sew 2 half blocks, 3 blocks, and 8 side setting triangles to make the middle row. Press the seam allowances toward the setting triangles.

Middle row
Make 1

3. Join the 3 rows.

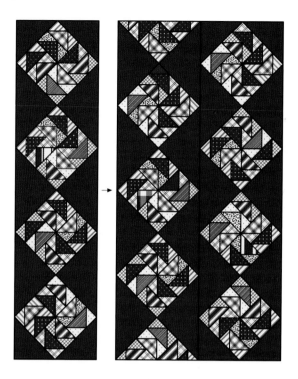

4. Layer the quilt top with batting and backing; baste. Quilt as desired, or follow the quilting suggestion on page 111. (See "Finishing Techniques" on pages 102–109.)

5. Bind the edges with bias strips of fabric.

Free Trade

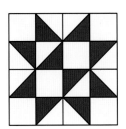

Dimensions: *68¹/₂" x 68¹/₂"*
Finished Block Size: *10" x 10"*

16 blocks, set 4 across and 4 down with 2¹/₂"-wide sashing and bias-square cornerstones; 8"-wide border.

Materials: 44"-wide fabric

⅝ yd. *each* of 8 navy blue prints with light backgrounds
8 fat quarters (18" x 22") dark navy blue prints
2⅛ yds. navy blue print for border (cut along the lengthwise grain)
4¹/₄ yds. for backing
¹/₂ yd. for 284" (7⅞ yds.) of bias binding

TIPS FOR FABRIC SELECTION: Select a variety of navy blue prints. Mix and match the light print backgrounds with the dark navy blue prints as you make each set of bias squares for the blocks. Cut sashing from a variety of light prints and dark navy blue prints. Place the light-background and dark-background sashing rows so they form alternating diagonal bands of color. Arrange the bias-square sashing squares to continue the color bands.

Cutting

From EACH light-background print, cut:
  12 squares, each 3" x 3" (cut 6 matching squares for each block).
  3 rectangles, each 3" x 10¹/₂", for a total of 20 sashing strips.
  1 rectangle, 12" x 16", for bias squares.
From EACH dark navy blue fat quarter, cut:
  3 rectangles, each 3" x 10¹/₂", for a total of 20 sashing strips.
  1 rectangle, 12" x 16", for bias squares.
From border fabric, cut:
  2 strips, each 8¹/₄" x 53", along the lengthwise grain of fabric, for side borders.
  2 strips, each 8¹/₄" x 68¹/₂", along the lengthwise grain of fabric, for top and bottom borders.

Block Assembly

1. Pair each of the 12" x 16" light-background rectangles with a 12" x 16" dark navy blue rectangle, *right sides up.* Cut and sew together 2³/₄"-wide bias strips, following the directions for making bias squares on pages 25–27. Cut a total of 24 bias squares, each 3" x 3", from each strip-pieced fabric combination. Use 10 matching bias squares (160 total) for each block and 25 bias squares for sashing squares.

Cut 185 total.

2. Arrange and sew together 6 matching light-background squares with 10 matching bias squares to make each Free Trade block. Take care to place each bias square's angle correctly.

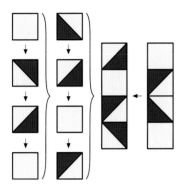 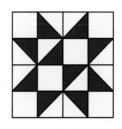

Make 16

Quilt Top Assembly and Finishing

1. Arrange blocks, sashing strips, and the bias squares used for sashing squares. Arrange the colors so that each block is surrounded by 2 light-background and 2 dark-background sashing strips. Be sure to rotate the bias squares as necessary to continue the line of the light and dark sashing strips.
2. Sew the units into rows. Press the seams toward the sashing strips. Sew the rows together.
3. Add the 8$\frac{1}{4}$"-wide navy blue border strips, following the directions for borders with straight-cut corners on page 102.
4. Layer the quilt top with batting and backing; baste. Quilt as desired, or follow the quilting suggestion on page 112. (See "Finishing Techniques" on pages 102–109.)
5. Bind the edges with bias strips of fabric.

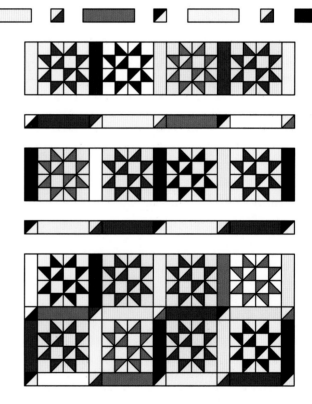

MADE IN JAPAN, *pieced by Nancy J. Martin, 1993, Woodinville, Washington, 68½" x 68½".*
These Free Trade blocks are made from reproduction indigo prints. The quilt name was inspired by
the APEC trade talks, which were taking place in Seattle when the blocks were being made.
Quilted by Alvina Nelson, Salina, Kansas. (Collection of That Patchwork Place, Inc.)

Grape Basket

Dimensions: 58½" x 58½"
Finished Block Size: 10" x 10"

9 blocks, set diagonally with alternate blocks; 8"-wide outer border.

Materials: 44"-wide fabric

9 fat eighths (9" x 22") light-background fabric for blocks and bias squares
5 fat eighths (9" x 22") dark purple fabrics for blocks
1¼ yds. light print for set pieces and alternate blocks
1⅞ yds. dark purple for border
9 squares, each 7" x 7", of medium purple for bias squares
3¾ yds. fabric for backing
½ yd. for 244" (6⅞ yds.) of bias binding

TIP FOR FABRIC SELECTION: Mix and match the light bias squares with the dark bias squares and basket fabrics, using the same background fabric within each block. See page 27 for cutting just a few bias squares, since only 4 dark bias squares are needed for each basket.

Cutting

From EACH fat quarter of light-background fabric, cut:
   1 square, 7" x 7", for medium purple bias squares.
   1 triangle, 7" along each short side, for dark purple bias squares.

   1 square, 4⅞" x 4⅞". Cut once diagonally to make 2 triangles.
   2 rectangles, each 2½" x 6½".
   1 square, 2½" x 2½".
From EACH dark purple fat eighth, cut:
   1 square, 7" x 7". Cut once diagonally for 2 triangles to make dark purple bias squares.
   1 square, 4⅞" x 4⅞". Cut once diagonally to make 2 triangles (10 total—only 9 are needed).
   2 squares, each 2⅞" x 2⅞". Cut each square once diagonally to make 4 triangles (20 triangles total).
From light print, cut:
   2 squares, each 15½" x 15½". Cut each square twice diagonally to make 8 side setting triangles.
   4 squares, each 10½" x 10½", for alternate blocks.
   2 squares, each 8" x 8". Cut each square once diagonally to make 4 corner setting triangles.
From dark purple fabric for border, cut from the lengthwise grain:
   2 strips, each 8¼" x 42½", for side borders.
   2 strips, each 8¼" x 58½", for top and bottom borders.

VINTAGE WINE, pieced by Cleo Nollette, 1994, Seattle, Washington, 58¹/₂" x 58¹/₂".
A collection of purple fabrics, including bedding fabric purchased in Holland, lends excitement to this scrappy quilt.
Quilted by Mrs. Abe Yoder, Holmes County, Ohio. (Collection of That Patchwork Place, Inc.)

Block Assembly

1. To make medium purple bias squares, pair each of the light-background 7" squares with a medium purple 7" square, *right sides up*. Cut and sew together $2\frac{1}{2}$"-wide bias strips, following the directions for making just a few bias squares on page 27. Cut 7 bias squares, each $2\frac{1}{2}$" x $2\frac{1}{2}$", from each fabric combination, for a total of 63 bias squares. Save leftovers for another project.

Make 63

2. To make dark purple bias squares, pair each light-background triangle with a dark purple triangle, *right sides up*. Cut the unit into $2\frac{1}{2}$"-wide bias strips, measuring from the long bias edge.

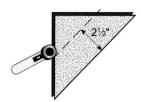

3. Stitch the strips together as shown. Then cut 4 bias squares, each $2\frac{1}{2}$" x $2\frac{1}{2}$", from each fabric combination for a total of 36.

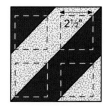

4. Arrange the units and sew together, following the piecing diagram.

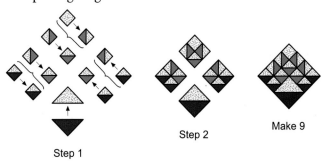

Step 1

Step 2

Make 9

5. Complete the block as shown.

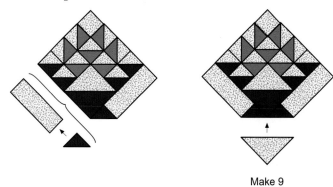

Make 9

Quilt Top Assembly and Finishing

1. Arrange and sew Grape Basket blocks, alternate blocks, and setting triangles into diagonal rows. Press the seam allowances away from the pieced blocks. Sew the rows together. Add a corner setting triangle to each corner.

2. Add $8\frac{1}{4}$"-wide dark purple strips for the border, following the directions for borders with straight-cut corners on page 102.
3. Layer the quilt top with batting and backing; baste. Quilt as desired, or follow the quilting suggestion on page 112. (See "Finishing Techniques" on pages 102–109.)
4. Bind the edges with bias strips of fabric.

Mystery Block

BLOCK A   BLOCK B

Dimensions: 82¾" x 105¼"
Finished Block Size: 5⅝" x 5⅝"

252 blocks, with 2 colorations, set 14 across and 18 down; 2"-wide borders.

Materials: 44"-wide fabric

1 yd. *each* of 6 dark-background red, purple, and burgundy prints for blocks

1 yd. *each* of 6 light-background red, purple, and burgundy prints for blocks

⅞ yd. burgundy print for borders

7¼ yds. fabric for backing

⅔ yd. for 386" (10¾ yds.) of bias binding

TIPS FOR FABRIC SELECTION: To achieve an old-fashioned look, don't overmatch the colors selected. For added variety, be sure to include tiny dots, stripes, and prints, such as those used in shirts.

Cutting

From dark-background prints, cut:

23 strips, each 3¾" wide. Cut the strips into 252 squares, each 3¾" x 3¾". Cut each square once diagonally to make 504 triangles for Triangle H.

18 strips, each 2⅞" wide. Cut the strips into 252 squares, each 2⅞" x 2⅞". Cut each square once diagonally to make 504 triangles for Triangle C.

14 strips, each 2¼" wide. Cut the strips into 252 squares, each 2¼" x 2¼". Cut each square once diagonally to make 504 triangles for Triangle F.

8 strips, each 2½" wide. Cut the strips into 126 squares, each 2½" x 2½", for Square A.

From light-background prints, cut:

23 strips, each 3¾" wide. Cut the strips into 252 squares, each 3¾" x 3¾". Cut each square once diagonally to make 504 triangles for Triangle D.

18 strips, each 2⅞" wide. Cut the strips into 252 squares, each 2⅞" x 2⅞". Cut each square once diagonally to make 504 triangles for Triangle G.

14 strips, each 2¼" wide. Cut the strips into 252 squares, each 2¼" x 2¼". Cut each square once diagonally to make 504 triangles for Triangle B.

8 strips, each 2½" wide. Cut the strips into 126 squares, each 2½" x 2½", for Square E.

From burgundy print for border, cut:

12 strips, each 2¼" wide.

Block Assembly

1. Using Square A and dark and light Triangles B, C, and D, piece 126 Mystery blocks with the Block A coloration. Press triangles away from the center. Trim the block to measure 6⅛" x 6⅛".

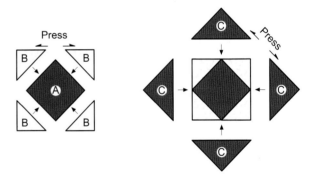

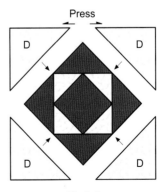

Block A
Make 126

2. Using Square E and light and dark Triangles F, G, and H, piece 126 Mystery blocks with the Block B coloration. Press triangles away from the center. Trim the block to measure $6\frac{1}{8}$" x $6\frac{1}{8}$".

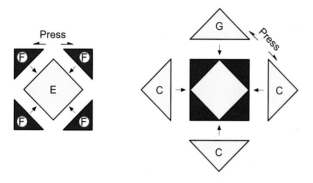

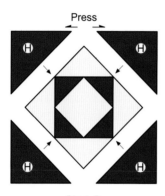

Block B
Make 126

Quilt Top Assembly and Finishing

1. Refering to the illustration below, sew the blocks into 18 rows of 14 blocks each, alternating 7 A blocks with 7 B blocks. Alternate A and B blocks at the beginning of rows. Sew the rows together.

2. Add $2\frac{1}{4}$"-wide burgundy strips for the border, following the directions for borders with straight-cut corners on page 102.

3. Layer the quilt top with batting and backing; baste. Quilt as desired, or follow the quilting suggestion on page 112. (See "Finishing Techniques" on pages 102–109.)

4. Bind the edges with bias strips of fabric.

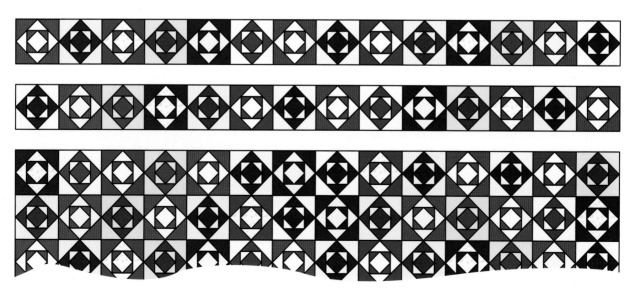

Make 18 rows.

MYSTERY QUILT, *maker unknown, Nebraska, ca. 1910, 82¾" x 105¼".*
This charming quilt, purchased at a garage sale, alternates two colorations of the same block in a
"Robbing Peter to Pay Paul" style. (Collection of Carol Dunklau.)

Star and Chain

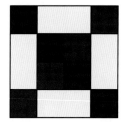

STAR BLOCK   **CHAIN BLOCK**

Dimensions: 57¼" x 68½"
Finished Block Size: 8" x 8"

12 Star blocks, set diagonally with 20 Chain blocks, each 8" x 8"; side and corner setting pieces; 6"-wide outer border.

Materials: 44"-wide fabric

2¼ yds. beige background for blocks
1¾ yds. black print for chain and border (cut along the lengthwise grain)
1 fat quarter (18" x 22") large-scale black print for star centers and chain
4 fat eighths (9" x 22") purple fabrics for chain
1 fat quarter pink print for star tips
1 fat quarter green print for star tips
1 fat quarter black print for black chain
3⅝ yds. fabric for backing
½ yd. fabric for 262" (7¼ yds.) bias binding

TIPS FOR FABRIC SELECTION: Select a light-background fabric for the corners of the Star block and the edges of the Chain block. These two pieces blend together when the alternate blocks are sewn side by side. The large-scale print in the center of the Star block is surrounded by star tips from either pink or green prints. Purple prints form a vertical chain across the quilt. The black prints make the horizontal chain.

Cutting

From beige background fabric, cut:
2 strips, each 5¼" wide. Cut the strips into 12 squares, each 5¼" x 5¼". Cut each square twice diagonally to make 48 triangles.
3 strips, each 2½" wide. Cut the strips into 48 squares, each 2½" x 2½".

5 strips, each 4½" wide. Cut the strips into 80 rectangles, each 2½" x 4½".
4 squares, each 12¾" x 12¾". Cut each square twice diagonally to make 14 side setting triangles (there will be 2 left over).
2 squares, each 6¾" x 6¾". Cut each square once diagonally to make 4 corner setting triangles.

From black print for the border, cut along the lengthwise grain:
2 strips, each 6¼" x 56½", for side borders.
2 strips, each 6¼" x 57¼", for top and bottom borders.

From large-scale black print fat quarter, cut:
12 squares, each 4½" x 4½", for the star centers.

From EACH purple fat eighth, cut:
20 squares, each 2½" x 2½", for the purple chain, for a total of 80 squares.

From EACH pink and green fat quarter, cut:
24 squares, each 2⅞" x 2⅞". Cut each square once diagonally to make 48 triangles for the star tips (96 triangles total).

Additional Cutting

From the black fabrics, cut
80 squares total, each 2½" x 2½", for the black chain.

Block Assembly

1. Join the units to make 12 Star blocks.

Make 24 pink.
Make 24 green.

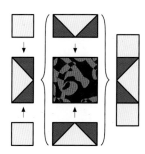
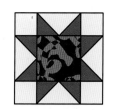

Make 6 with pink star tips.
Make 6 with green star tips.

*ELECTRIC SKY, pieced by Nancy J. Martin, 1993, Woodinville, Washington, 57¼" x 68½".
A coordinating collection of purple and black fabrics unites this energetic design.
Quilted by Sue von Jentzen, Granite Falls, Washington. (Collection of That Patchwork Place, Inc.)*

2. Join the units to make 20 Chain blocks.

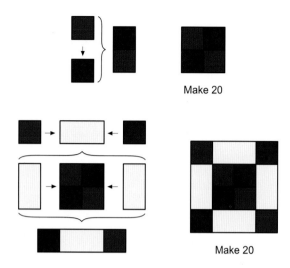

Make 20

Make 20

Quilt Top Assembly and Finishing

1. Sew the blocks into diagonal rows, alternating pink and green Star blocks with Chain blocks. Sew a side setting triangle at each row end. Sew the rows together. Sew corner setting triangles to the corners of the quilt top.

2. Add 6¼"-wide black print strips for the border, following the directions for borders with straight-cut corners on page 102.

3. Layer the quilt top with batting and backing; baste. Quilt as desired, or follow the quilting suggestion on page 113. (See "Finishing Techniques" on pages 102–109.)

4. Bind the edges with bias strips of fabric.

Chimneys and Cornerstones

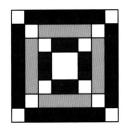

Dimensions: 100" x 109"
Finished Block Size: 8" x 8"

132 blocks, set 11 blocks x 12 blocks with 1"-wide sashing and cornerstones.

Materials: 44"-wide fabric

3⅝ yds. muslin for center squares and cornerstones
¼ yd. *each* of 8 red prints for blocks (Round 1)
½ yd. *each* of 8 tan prints for blocks (Round 2)
½ yd. *each* of 8 brown prints for blocks (Round 3)
⅜ yd. *each* of 8 dark red prints for sashing
9 yds. fabric for backing
¾ yd. fabric for 428" (11⅞ yds.) bias binding

TIPS FOR FABRIC SELECTION: A variety of prints, selected from each color family, gives this quilt a scrappy look. Red prints for Round 1, tan prints for Round 2, and brown prints for Round 3 are highlighted by each block's muslin centers and cornerstones. Dark red sashing accents each block, and muslin cornerstones link the blocks by forming a chain across the quilt top.

Cutting

From muslin, cut:

9 strips, each 2½" wide. Cut the strips into 132 squares, each 2½" x 2½", for center of each block.

57 strips, each 1½" wide. Cut the strips into 1,584 squares, each 1½" x 1½", for block corner stones.

6 strips, each 1½" wide. Cut the strips into 156 squares, each 1½" x 1½", for sashing corner stones.

From red prints for Round 1, cut:

19 strips total, each 2½" wide. Cut the strips into 528 rectangles, each 1½" x 2½".

From tan prints for Round 2, cut:

19 strips total, each 4½" wide. Cut the strips into 528 rectangles, each 1½" x 4½".

From brown prints for Round 3, cut:

19 strips total, each 6½" wide. Cut the strips into 528 rectangles, each 1½" x 6½".

From dark red prints for the sashing, cut:

11 strips total, each 8½" wide. Cut the strips into 287 rectangles, each 1½" x 8½".

Block Assembly

1. To make Round 1, sew the red rectangles and muslin cornerstones to the block center.

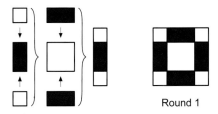

Round 1

2. To make Round 2, sew the tan rectangles and muslin cornerstones to Round 1.

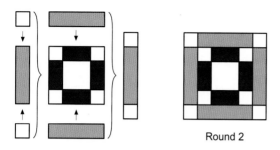

Round 2

3. To make Round 3, sew the brown rectangles and muslin cornerstones to Round 2.

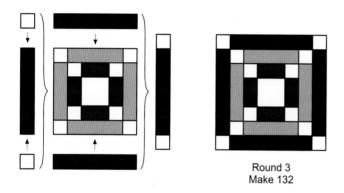

Round 3
Make 132

Quilt Top Assembly and Finishing

1. Referring to the illustration below, stitch 11 blocks and 12 dark red sashing strips into a row. Stitch 12 cornerstones and 11 dark red sashing strips into a row.
2. Alternate the sashing rows with rows of blocks and stitch together.
3. Layer the quilt top with batting and backing; baste. Quilt as desired, or follow the quilting suggestion on page 113. (See "Finishing Techniques" on pages 102–109.)
4. Bind the edges with bias strips of fabric.

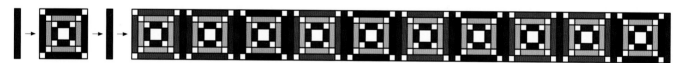

Make 12 rows.

Make 13 rows.

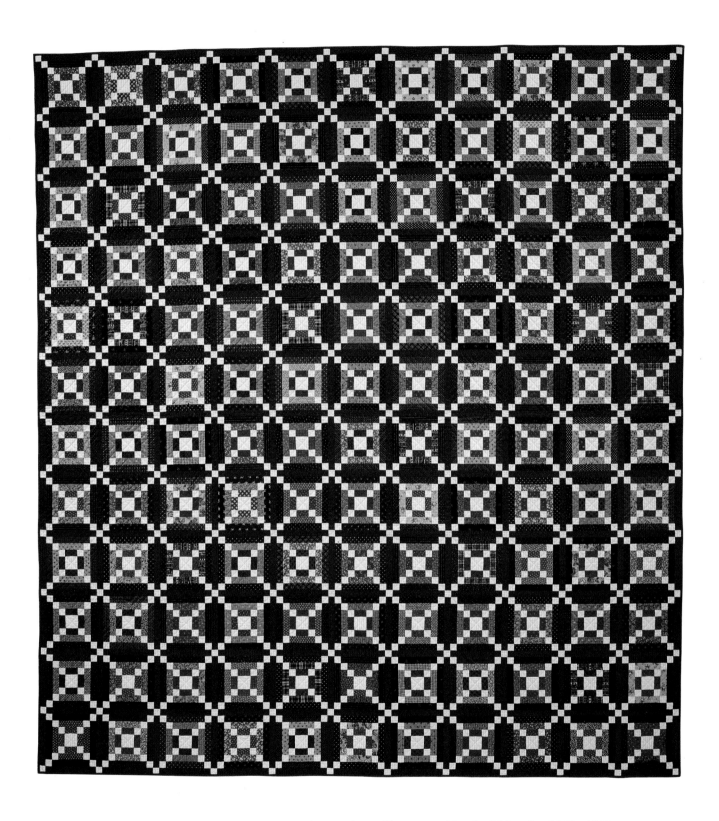

CHIMNEYS AND CORNERSTONES, *by Carol Dunklau, 1989, Lincoln, Nebraska, 100" x 109".*
This wonderful scrap quilt skillfully combines an assortment of tan, brown, and red fabrics. Carol's quilt won first place at the 1989 Nebraska State Fair and Best of Show at Quilt America in Indianapolis in 1991.

Double Cross

Dimensions: 72½" x 72½"
Finished Block Size: 10" x 10"

16 blocks, framed with 4 corner triangles, set 4 across and 4 down; 8"-wide outer border with mitered corners.

Materials: 44"-wide fabric

8 fat quarters (18" x 22") light rose prints for blocks
8 fat quarters medium rose prints for blocks
½ yd. *each* of 8 dark rose prints for blocks
2¼ yds. striped rose for borders (Cut along the lengthwise grain)
4⅝ yds. fabric for backing
½ yd. fabric for 300" (8⅜ yds.) bias binding (or use leftover border fabric)

TIPS FOR FABRIC SELECTION: Select a variety of light, medium, and dark rose prints. Mix and match to make 8 identical pairs of 10" x 10" blocks. To add variety, use medium and dark rose corner triangles to frame the blocks and create an on-point set. Using a striped fabric for the wide border emphasizes the mitered corners.

Cutting

From EACH fat quarter of light rose print, cut:
   2 squares, each 8" x 8", for bias squares (Unit C).
   2 squares, each 7" x 7", for bias squares (Unit B).
   4 squares, each 3¾" x 3¾". Cut each square twice diagonally to make 16 triangles, for a total of 128 triangles (Triangle A).
From EACH fat quarter of medium rose print, cut:
   2 squares, each 8" x 8". Cut each square once diagonally for a total of 4 triangles. You need a total of 32 corner setting triangles from medium rose fabric.
   1 square, 9" x 9", to make bias squares for .5 units.
   2 squares, each 5½" x 5½", for block centers (Square D).

From EACH dark rose print, cut:
   2 squares, each 8" x 8". Cut each square once diagonally for a total of 4 triangles. You need a total of 32 corner setting triangles from dark rose fabric.
   2 squares, each 8" x 8", for bias squares (Unit C).
   2 squares, each 7" x 7", for bias squares (Unit B).
   1 square, 9" x 9", to make bias squares for .5 units.
From striped rose for border, cut:
   4 strips, each 8¼" x 75", along the lengthwise grain of fabric.

Block Assembly

NOTE: For each block, use matching pairs of light and dark rose 7" squares to make the bias squares for Units B and C.

1. To make Unit B bias squares, pair 7" light rose and dark rose squares, *right sides up*. Cut and sew together 2¼"-wide bias strips, following the directions for making just a few bias squares on page 27. Cut 8 bias squares, each 2¼" x 2¼". Repeat for each of the remaining light/dark pairs, for a total of 64 bias squares.

2¼"
Unit B
Make 64

2. To make .5 unit bias squares, pair 9" medium and dark rose squares, *right sides up*. Cut and sew together 3⅛"-wide bias strips for bias squares. Cut 8 bias squares, each 3⅜" x 3⅜". Cut each bias square once diagonally to make a .5 unit. Repeat for each of the remaining medium-and-dark pairs, for a total of 128 units.

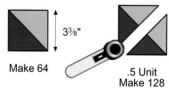

3⅜"
Make 64
.5 Unit
Make 128

3. To make Unit C bias squares, pair 8" light and dark rose squares, *right sides up*. Cut and sew together 2¾"-wide bias strips for bias squares. From each combination, cut 8 bias squares, each 3" x 3". Repeat with each of the remaining light-and-dark pairs, for a total of 64 bias squares.

3"
Unit C
Make 64

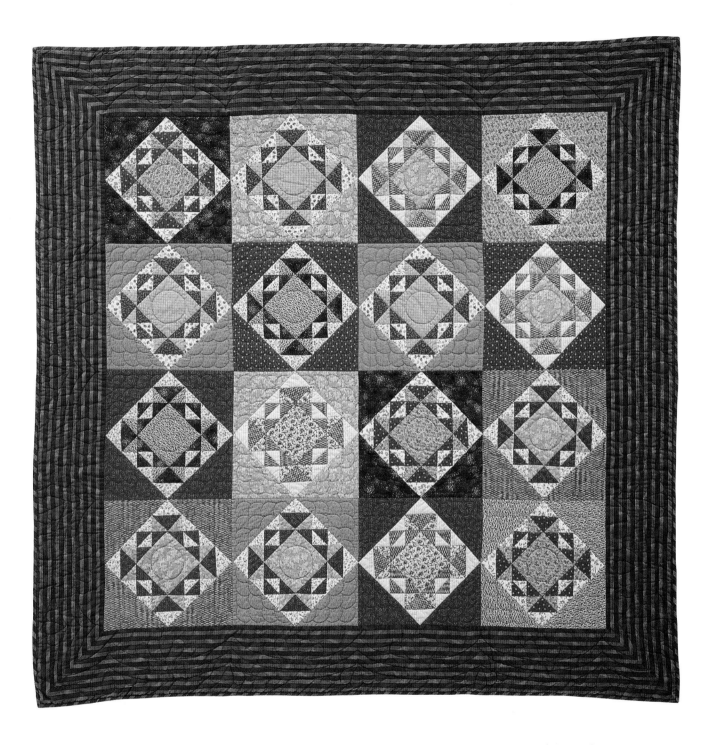

ROSY RASPBERRY, pieced by Nancy J. Martin, 1993, Woodinville, Washington, 72½" x 72½".
This traditional block, once known as "Flower Pot," is made from a collection of pink and rose fabrics,
which were selected by Judy Pollard. A circular quilting pattern softens and enhances the corners of each block.
Quilted by Nancy Sweeney, Camano Island, Washington. (Collection of That Patchwork Place, Inc.)

4. Sew light rose triangles to Unit B bias squares.

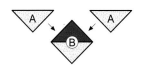

Make 4 for each block.

5. Sew a .5 unit to each side.

.5 unit   .5 unit

Make 4 for each block.

6. Sew a unit made in step 5 to each side of a 5½" x 5½" Square D. Use matching medium rose fabrics for .5 units and Square D.

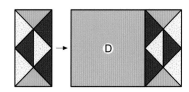

Make 1 for each block.

7. Sew a Unit C bias square to each side of a unit made in step 5.

Make 2 for each block.

8. Join the units to complete the block.

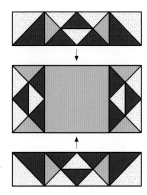 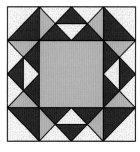

Make 16

9. Sew matching corner setting triangles to each side of the block.

Quilt Top Assembly and Finishing

1. Sew the blocks together in 4 rows of 4 each, alternating medium and dark blocks. Sew the rows together to form the quilt top.

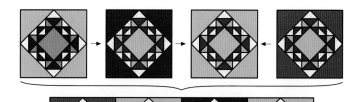

2. Add the 8¼"-wide striped rose borders, following the directions for "Borders with Mitered Corners" on page 79.
3. Layer the quilt top with batting and backing; baste. Quilt as desired, or follow the quilting suggestion on page 113. (See "Finishing Techniques" on pages 102–109.)
4. Bind the edges with bias strips of fabric.

Borders with Mitered Corners

1. Measure through the center of the quilt top from top to bottom and subtract 1/2" for seam allowances. Double the width of the border and add this figure to the measurement; cut the side borders to this length. Do not add borders to the quilt yet.

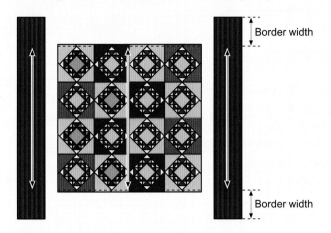

2. Repeat step 1 for the top and bottom borders, measuring the quilt from side to side.

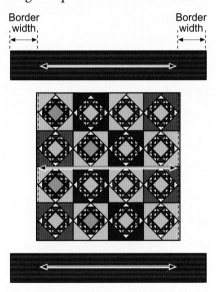

3. Mark the centers and quarter points of both the quilt edges and the border strips. Pin the borders to the quilt top. Stitch each border to the quilt top, starting and stopping 1/4" from the edges of the quilt top.

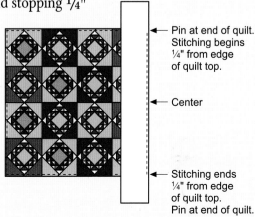

Pin at end of quilt. Stitching begins 1/4" from edge of quilt top.

Center

Stitching ends 1/4" from edge of quilt top. Pin at end of quilt.

4. At the ironing board, place the quilt right side up, overlapping borders as shown.

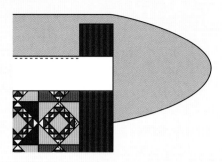

5. Fold back the border, making a 45°-angle fold. Press the fold to crease it and pin the ends of the borders together.

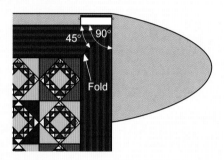

45°   90°

Fold

6. Carefully turn the quilt over. Pin, then stitch the borders together along the crease. Begin stitching at the seam line where the borders join the quilt.

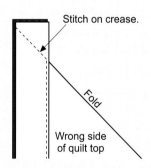

Stitch on crease.

Fold

Wrong side of quilt top

7. Trim, leaving a 1/4"-wide seam allowance. Press the seam open. Repeat for the remaining corners.

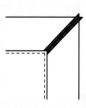

Love Chain

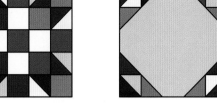

SISTER'S CHOICE BLOCK   CHAIN BLOCK

Dimensions: 84" x 84"
Finished Block Size: 10" x 10"

49 blocks, 24 Sister's Choice blocks alternate with 25 Chain blocks, set 7 across and 7 down; 1"-wide inner border and 6"-wide outer border.

Materials: 44"-wide fabric

⅜ yd. *each* of 10 different navy blue prints

1 yd. *each* of 5 tan prints for background and bias squares

¼ yd. *each* of 4 light-background prints for Ninepatches

5 fat quarters (18" x 22") of assorted rusty red fabrics for bias squares

1 square, 10" x 10", of rusty red for bias squares

½ yd. rust print for inner border

2 yds. navy blue print for outer border

⅝ yd. navy blue for 346" (9⅝ yds.) bias binding

TIPS FOR FABRIC SELECTION: Choose several tan prints for the main piece of the Chain block. The Sister's Choice blocks have Ninepatch centers made of dark- and light-background navy blue prints. Use assorted tan prints and rusty red prints to make the bias squares for both blocks. Alternate Sister's Choice blocks with Chain blocks to form an overall pattern, called Love Chain, across the quilt top. This pattern was first published in *Hearth and Home* magazine in 1917 under the name "Atlanta."

Cutting

From EACH navy blue print, cut:

2 strips, each 2½" wide. Reserve 8 strips for Ninepatches. Cut 12 of the strips into 192 squares, each 2½" x 2½", for the Sister's Choice blocks.

1 strip, 2⅞" wide. Cut the strip into 10 squares, each 2⅞" x 2⅞". Cut each square once diagonally to make a total of 200 triangles for the Chain blocks.

From EACH tan print, cut:

1 fat quarter for bias squares, 18" x 22".

5 squares, each 10½" x 10½", for a total of 25 squares. See step 9 on page 82 for additional cutting instructions.

From ONE of the tan prints, cut:

1 square, 10" x 10", for bias squares.

From the light-background prints, cut a total of:

7 strips, each 2½" wide, for Ninepatches.

From rust print for the inner border, cut:

8 strips, each 1½" wide.

From navy blue print for the outer border, cut:

10 strips, each 6¼" wide.

Block Assembly

1. To make ninepatch units, sew 2 of the 2½"-wide assorted navy blue strips, to a 2½"-wide light-background strip to make a 6½"-wide strip-pieced unit. Cut each strip-pieced unit into 16 segments, each 2½" wide.

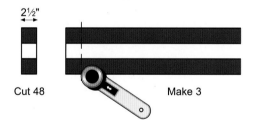

Cut 48   Make 3

2. Sew 2 of the assorted light-background strips, each 2½"-wide, to a 2½"-wide navy blue strip to make a 6½"-wide strip-pieced unit. From each strip-pieced unit, cut 2½"-wide segments.

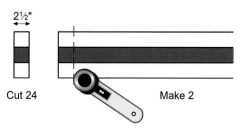

Cut 24   Make 2

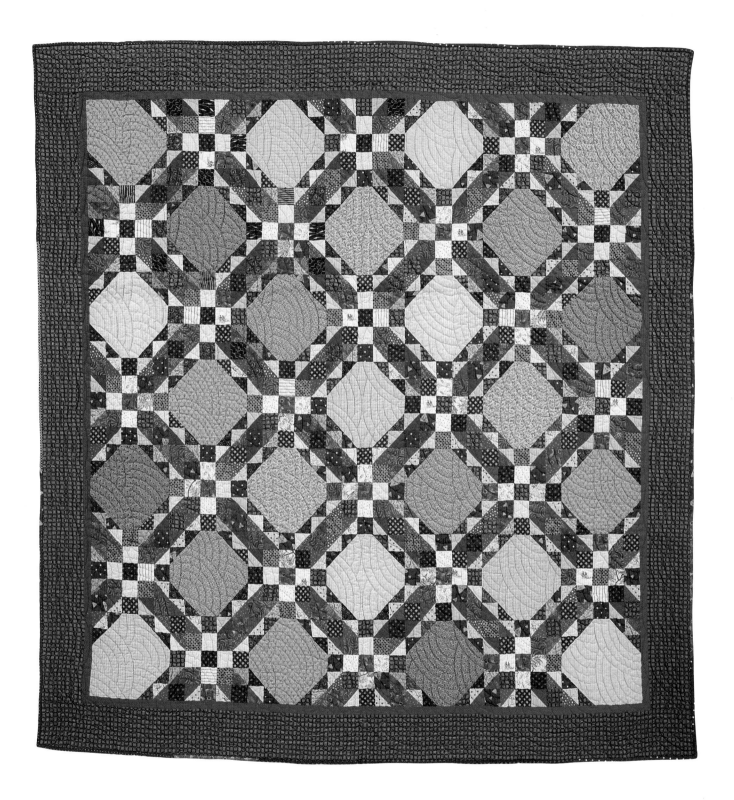

LOVE CHAIN, pieced by Nancy J. Martin, 1993, Woodinville, Washington, 84" x 84".
Two traditional blocks pieced in an old-fashioned color scheme give a mellow look to this quilt.
A fan quilting pattern unifies the quilt and softens the angular corners of the block.
Quilted by Mrs. Andy A. Yoder, Holmes County, Ohio. (Collection of That Patchwork Place, Inc.)

3. Join the segments to make 24 ninepatch units.

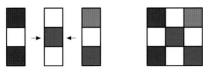

Make 24

4. To make bias squares, pair each of the 5 tan fat quarters with a rusty-red fat quarter, *right sides up*. Pair the 10" tan square with the 10" rusty-red square. Cut and sew together 2½"-wide bias strips, following the directions for making bias squares on pages 25–27. Cut 56 bias squares, each 2½" x 2½", from each fat quarter combination. Cut 12 bias squares from the 10" squares, for a total of 292 bias squares.

2½"

Make 292

5. Sew a bias square to each side of a navy blue square.

Make 96

6. Sew a unit made in step 5 to opposite sides of each ninepatch unit.

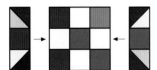 

Make 24

7. Sew a navy blue square to each end of the units made in step 5.

Make 48

8. Join the remaining units to complete the Sister's Choice block.

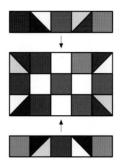 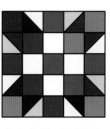

Sister's Choice Block
Make 24

9. Using the template for trimming on page 83, trim the corners of each 10½" tan square.

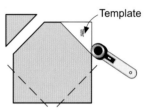

Template

Make 25

10. Sew a navy blue triangle to the light sides of the remaining bias squares. Sew 1 of these units to each corner of a trimmed tan square to make the Chain blocks.

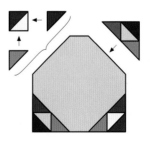

Chain Block
Make 25

Quilt Top Assembly and Finishing

1. Join 4 Chain blocks with 3 Sister's Choice blocks to make Row A.

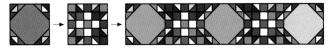

Row A
Make 4

2. Join 4 Sister's Choice blocks with 3 Chain blocks to make Row B.

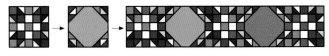

Row B
Make 3

3. Starting and ending with Row A, alternate Rows A and B to form the quilt top. Sew the rows together.

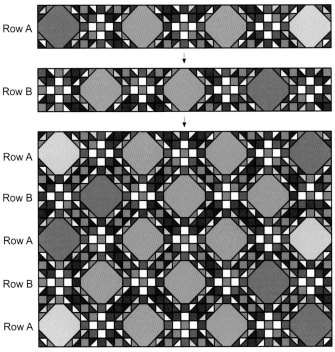

4. Add the 1½"-wide rust strips for the inner border and the 6¼"-wide navy blue strips for the outer border, following the directions for borders with straight-cut corners on page 102.

5. Layer the quilt top with batting and backing; baste. Quilt as desired, or follow the quilting suggestion on page 114. (See "Finishing Techniques" on pages 102–109.)

6. Bind the edges with bias strips of fabric.

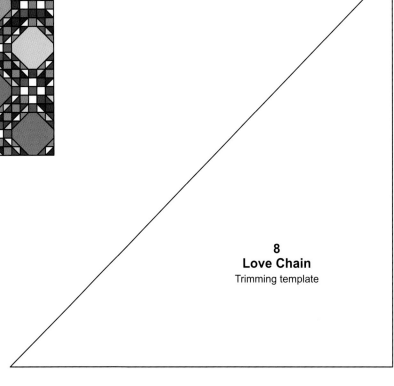

8
Love Chain
Trimming template

Ohio Star

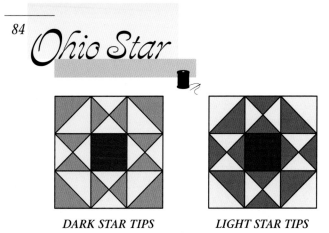

DARK STAR TIPS   LIGHT STAR TIPS

Dimensions: 50" x 50"
Finished Block Size: 9" x 9"

16 blocks, set 4 across and 4 down; 1"-wide inner border and 6"-wide outer border.

Materials: 44" wide fabric

8 fat quarters (18" x 22") blue prints with light backgrounds

8 fat quarters blue prints with dark backgrounds

4 fat eighths (9" x 22") contrasting red prints

1/4 yd. red print for inner border

1 1/2 yds. plaid for borders (cut along the lengthwise grain)

3 1/8 yds. fabric for backing

1/3 yd. fabric for 210" (5 7/8 yds.) bias binding (or use leftover border fabric)

TIPS FOR FABRIC SELECTION: Mix and match the light- and dark-background prints to make the Square 2 units for the Ohio Star blocks. When joining blocks, arrange the pieces so that half the stars have light tips and half have dark tips. Select deep red prints as accents for the star centers and inner border. Use a plaid for the outer border and binding.

Cutting

From EACH light- and dark-background fat quarter, cut:
2 squares, each 10" x 10", for bias squares.

From EACH fat eighth of red fabric, cut:
4 squares, each 3 1/2" x 3 1/2", for star centers.

From red print for border, cut:
2 strips, each 1 1/2" x 36 1/2".
2 strips, each 1 1/2" x 38 1/2".

From plaid, cut along the lengthwise grain:
2 strips, each 6 1/4" x 38 1/2", for side borders.
2 strips, each 6 1/4" x 50", for top and bottom borders.

Block Assembly

1. To make bias squares, pair 8 light- and 8 dark-background squares, *right sides up*. Cut and sew together 3 1/4"-wide bias strips, following the directions for making bias squares on pages 25–27. Cut 8 bias squares, each 3 1/2" x 3 1/2", from each fabric combination.

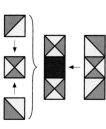
3 1/2"
Make 64

2. To make bias squares for Square 2 units, pair the 8 remaining 10" x 10" light- and dark-background squares, *right sides up*. Cut and sew together 3 1/2"-wide bias strips. Cut 8 bias squares, 3 7/8" x 3 7/8", from each fabric combination.

3 7/8"
Make 64

3. To make Square 2 units, place matching pairs of 3 7/8" bias squares together, right sides together. Place light triangles against dark triangles, nesting opposing seams. Cut each pair of bias squares once diagonally. Join these resulting triangle pairs with a 1/4"-wide seam. Press the seam open.

Place right sides together.   Second seam   Square 2 units Make 64

4. Arrange and sew together matching light- and dark-background fabrics for the pieced squares in each block.
Make 8 blocks with light star tips and 8 blocks with dark star tips.

Make 8 with light star tips.
Make 8 with dark star tips.

Quilt Top Assembly and Finishing

1. Join the blocks into 4 rows of 4 blocks each, alternating blocks with light and dark star tips as shown in the photo on page 85.

2. Add 1 1/2"-wide red strips for the inner border and 6 1/4"-wide plaid strips for the outer border. (See borders with straight-cut corners on page 102.)

3. Layer the quilt top with batting and backing; baste. Quilt as desired, or follow the quilting suggestion on page 114. (See "Finishing Techniques" on pages 102–109.)

4. Bind the edges with bias strips of fabric.

*OHIO STAR, pieced by Nancy J. Martin, 1993, Woodinville, Washington, 50" x 50".
A dark, rich color scheme, surrounded by a plaid border, gives this wall hanging a masculine feel.
Quilted by Donna K. Gundlach, Olympia, Washington. (Collection of That Patchwork Place, Inc.)*

Christmas Wreath

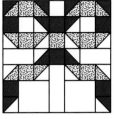 

BLOCK A BLOCK B

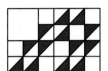 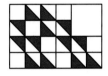

BLOCK C BLOCK D

Dimensions: 36" x 46"
Finished Block Sizes
    Block A: 14" x 14"
    Block B: 12" x 12"
    Blocks C and D: 8" x 12"

    1 Ribbon block, 2 blocks and 2 partial blocks, combined with setting pieces in a vertical setting; 2"-wide inner border and 3"-wide outer border.

Materials: 44"-wide fabric

1⅝ yds. white-on-white fabric for background and inner border
1 fat eighth (9" x 22") *each* of a dark red and a light red print for bow
1 fat eighth *each* of 5 dark green prints for wreath
½ yd. plaid for border
1½ yds. fabric for backing
⅓ yd. for 174" (4⅞ yds.) bias binding

TIPS FOR FABRIC SELECTION: Select a white tone-on-tone print for the background and an assortment of dark green prints for the wreath. Use two red prints for the bow, one light and one dark. Surround the wreath with a perky plaid border.

Cutting

From white-on-white background fabric, cut:
    7 squares, each 9" x 9", for bias squares D, E, and M.
    4 strips, each 2½" wide, for inner borders.
    2 rectangles, each 6½" x 12½", for setting piece J.
    2 rectangles, each 2½" x 8½", for sashing piece K.
    1 rectangle, 2½" x 18½", for sashing piece L.
    1 rectangle, 2½" x 6½", for piece I.
    8 squares, each 4½" x 4½", for piece G.
    4 rectangles, each 2½" x 4½", for piece F.
    40 squares, each 2½" x 2½", for block and sashing piece B.
From dark red print, cut:
    1 square, 9" x 9", for bias square D.
    4 squares, each 2½" x 2½", for piece C.
From light red print, cut:
    1 square, 9" x 9", for bias square E.
    7 squares, each 2½" x 2½", for piece A.
    2 squares, each 2⅞" x 2⅞". Cut each square once diagonally to make 4 triangles for the upper corners of Block A.
From EACH dark green print, cut:
    1 square, 9" x 9", for bias squares M.
    1 square, 2½" x 2½", for piece H.
From EACH of 2 of the dark green prints, cut:
    1 square, 2⅞" x 2⅞". Cut once diagonally to make a total of 4 triangles for the upper corners of Block A.
From plaid fabric, cut:
    4 strips, each 3¼" wide.

Block Assembly

1. To make the light-red-and-background (E) and dark-red-and-background (D) bias squares, pair each of the light and dark red 9" squares with a background 9" square, *right sides up.* Cut and sew together 2½"-wide bias strips, following the directions for making just a few bias squares on page 27. Cut 8 bias squares, each 2½" x 2½", from the light red fabric combination, and 6 bias squares, each 2½" x 2½", from the dark red fabric combination. Save extra bias squares for a leftover project. See "Leftovers" on page 94.

Bias square E   Bias square D
Cut 8   Cut 8

CHRISTMAS WREATH, pieced by Nancy J. Martin, 1994, Woodinville, Washington, 36" x 46".
Inspired by a wall hanging by Jo Baxter of Lincoln, Nebraska, Nancy added the
traditional Ribbon block as a bow for this charming Christmas wreath.
Quilted by Mrs. Mervin Shetler, Holmes County, Ohio. (Collection of That Patchwork Place, Inc.)

2. To make the green-and-background bias squares (M), follow the directions and measurements given in step 1. Pair each green and remaining background 9" squares to make a total of 64 bias squares, each 2½" x 2½". Cut and save extra bias squares for a leftover project.

2½"

Bias square M
Cut 64

3. Sew together light red and green triangles to make the upper corners of the bow.

Make 4

4. Following the illustration below, arrange pieces to make Block A.

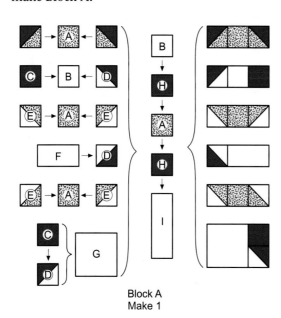

Block A
Make 1

5. Arrange and sew together 6 Units A and 3 Units B.

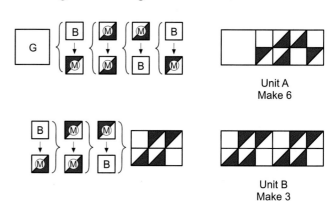

Unit A
Make 6

Unit B
Make 3

6. Sew together 2 Units A and 1 Unit B to make Block B. Take care to arrange the bias squares' angles and colors correctly.

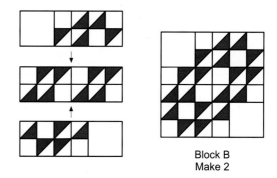

Block B
Make 2

7. Sew together remaining Units A and B to make Block C.

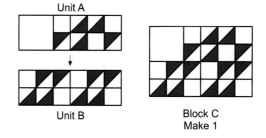

Unit A

Unit B

Block C
Make 1

8. Arrange and sew together Block D.

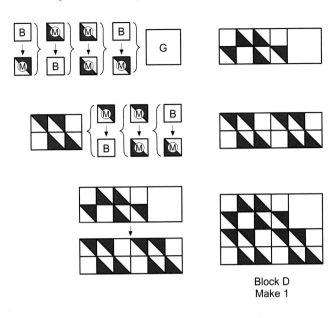

Block D
Make 1

9. Arrange and sew together setting pieces for each side of Block A.

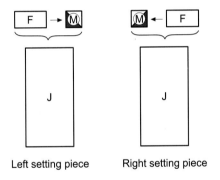

Left setting piece   Right setting piece

10. Assemble the sashing strips.

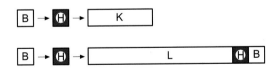

Quilt Top Assembly and Finishing

1. Sew a short pieced sashing strip made in step 10 between Blocks B, and Sashing Strip K between Blocks C and D, as shown. Sew a long pieced sashing strip made in step 10 between these sections. Sew a side setting piece made in step 9 to each side of Block A. Join the sections to form the quilt top.

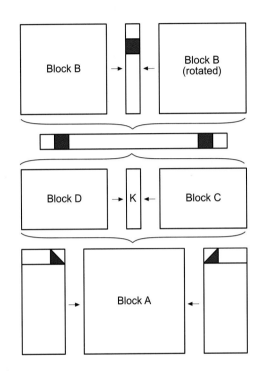

2. Add 2½"-wide background strips for the inner border and 3¼"-wide plaid strips for the outer border, following the directions for borders with straight-cut corners on page 102.
3. Layer the quilt top with batting and backing; baste. Quilt as desired, or follow the quilting suggestion on page 114. (See "Finishing Techniques" on pages 102–109.)
4. Bind the edges with bias strips of fabric.

Four by Four

© Sharyn Squier Craig

BLOCK (4 UNITS)   SINGLE UNIT

Dimensions: 88" x 100"
Finished Block Size: 8" x 8" (Single Unit: 4" x 4")

42 blocks, set 6 across and 7 down with sashing strips and 56 single-unit sashing squares; 2"-wide inner border, narrow piping, and 4"-wide outer border.

Materials: 44"-wide fabric

7¾ yds. black solid for blocks, sashing strips, and borders

1¾ yds. total of assorted bright fabrics (or 16 fat eighths, each 9" x 22", for a different fabric in each corner of each single unit)

1⅜ yds. dark floral print for block centers and narrow piping

7¾ yds. fabric for backing

⅔ yd. fabric for 386" (10¾ yds.) bias binding.

TIP FOR FABRIC PLACEMENT: Four of these 4" x 4" units set together led quilter Sharyn Squier Craig to name this pattern Four by Four. A dark floral print is used in the center of each unit and the narrow piping that accents the border. Black solid fabric is used for the remaining block pieces and for the sashing strips and borders. Select an assortment of bright prints for the corners of the block.

Cutting

From black solid fabric, cut:

10 strips, each 4¼" wide, for outer border.

9 strips, each 2½" wide, for inner border.

25 strips, each 4½" wide, for sashing.

28 strips, each 1½" wide, for Strip Row A.

17 strips, each 2½" wide, for Strip Row B.

From bright fabrics, cut:

34 strips, each 1½" wide, for Strip Row B.
(Cut 72 strips, each 1½" x 21", if you are using fat eighths.)

From dark floral print, cut:

14 strips, each 2½" wide, for Strip Row A.

9 strips, each ¾" wide, for piping.

Block Assembly

1. Sew a 1½"-wide black strip to each side of a 2½"-wide dark floral strip to make Strip Row A. The strip-pieced unit should measure 4½" wide when sewn. From these units, cut a total of 224 segments, each 2½" wide.

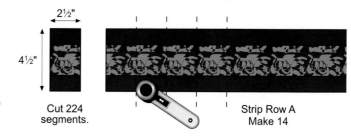

2½"

4½"

Cut 224 segments.

Strip Row A
Make 14

©Sharyn Squier Craig. Used with permission.

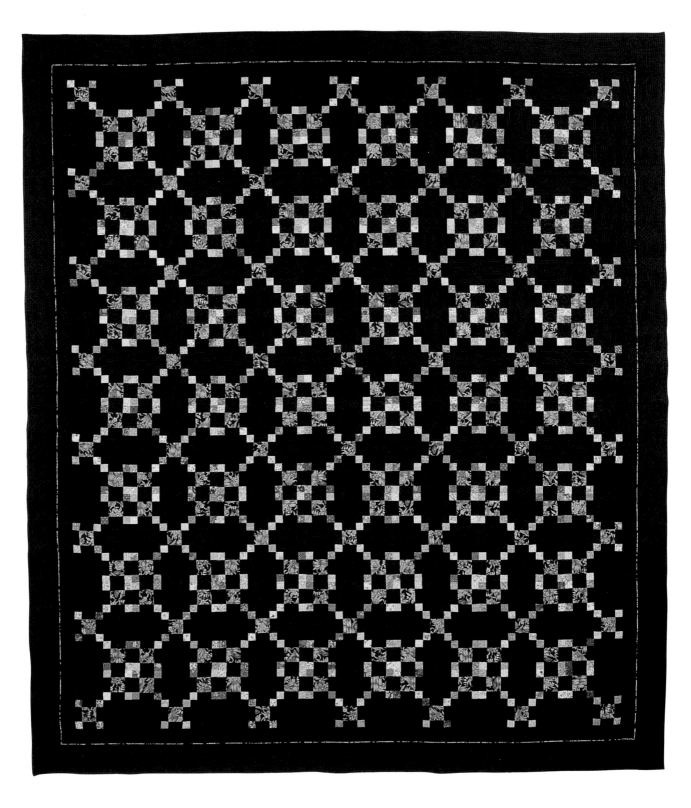

CITY LIGHTS, by Lonnie Henderson, 1993, Bainbridge Island, Washington, 88" x 100".
Lonnie was inspired by one of Sharyn Squier Craig's designs.
The dark background highlights the many fabrics as well as Lonnie's intricate quilting.
(Collection of Lonnie Henderson.)

2. Sew a 1½"-wide bright-fabric strip to each side of a 2½"-wide black strip to make Strip Row B. The strip-pieced unit should measure 4½" wide when sewn. From these units, cut a total of 448 segments, each 1½" wide.

NOTE: If you are using fat quarters or fat eighths, first cut each black strip in half crosswise, then randomly sew the 1½" x 21" bright-fabric strips to each side of the black strips.

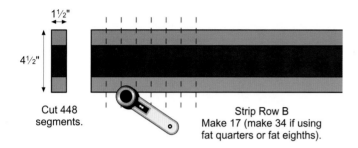

1½"

4½"

Cut 448 segments.

Strip Row B
Make 17 (make 34 if using fat quarters or fat eighths).

3. Sew a segment from Strip Row B to each side of a segment from Strip Row A to make a single unit.

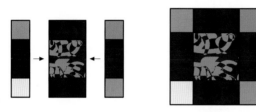

Make 224

4. Join 4 single units to make 42 Four by Four blocks.

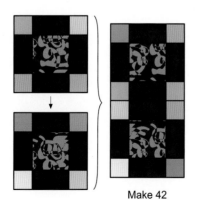

Make 42

Quilt Top Assembly

1. From the 4½"-wide black strips, cut 97 sashing strips, each 4½" x 8½".

8½"

4½"

Cut 97

2. Join 6 blocks and 7 sashing strips into a row. Make 7 of these rows. Press the seams toward the right end of the row.

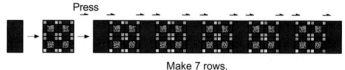

Press

Make 7 rows.

3. Join 7 single units and 6 sashing strips into a row. Make 8 of these rows. Press the seams toward the left end of the row.

Press

Make 8 rows.

4. Join the rows of blocks with sashing strips.

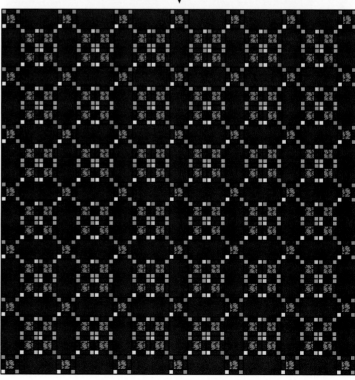

5. Add 2½"-wide black strips for the inner border, following the directions for borders with straight-cut corners on page 102.

6. Cut the ends of the ¾"-wide piping strips at a 45° angle and stitch together with a ¼"-wide seam allowance. Press the seam open.

7. Fold the continuous strip in half lengthwise, with wrong sides together and raw edges even. Press. Baste to the outside edge of the inner border. Be careful to maintain an even ¼"-wide seam allowance. Fold the corners to lie flat.

8. Add the 4¼"-wide black outer border with straight-cut corners, taking care not to catch the piping corners in the seams. Press seams toward the outer border.

9. Layer the quilt top with batting and backing; baste. Quilt as desired, or follow the quilting suggestion on page 115. (See "Finishing Techniques" on pages 102–109.)

10. Bind the edges with bias strips of fabric.

Raw edges

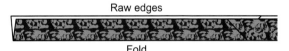

Fold

Raw edges

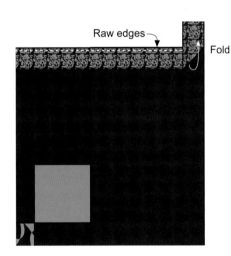

Fold

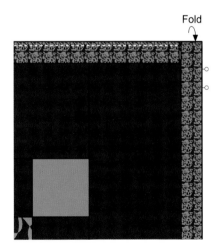

Fold

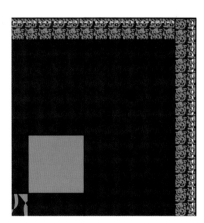

Just as those small dishes of leftover food nag at me every time I open the refrigerator door, so do those odds and ends of fabric left over from a quilt. The only difference is that I do something with the fabrics, while I end up disposing of the food (usually after it becomes an unrecognizable entity). The good thing about leftover or stored fabric is that it does not have an expiration date. It will always be there waiting for you.

The truth is, I am a compulsive finisher of projects. I will read to the end of a bad book, stick with an activity long after the joy has gone out of it, and finish a quilt even if I don't like it. I was raised in an era of "waste not, want not," which means I lie awake some nights thinking up ways to use certain scraps of fabric.

There is something inherently exciting about a true scrap project, a feeling of virtue akin to recycling garbage, bottles, paper, and cans. If you are of the same persuasion, the quilt patterns on the following pages should provide solutions to many of your scrap fabric problems. The format for these quilt directions varies from the rest of the book, since these quilts are meant to utilize your scraps. You can purchase new fabrics to include, but that's not the point of these quilts.

Each quilt design is given in a variety of sizes, to accommodate the amount of scraps that you have stored. Projects range in size from pillows and wall hangings to full-size quilts. Directions for finishing these quilts are found on pages 102–109. Use the information on page 108 to determine the amount of binding needed for your quilt project. Choose the size that corresponds to the amount of scraps and patience you have. Most of all, have fun!

For other quilt plans offering ways to use up your leftovers, check your local quilt shop or guild library for the following books published by That Patchwork Place:

Rotary Riot
   by Judy Hopkins and Nancy J. Martin
Rotary Roundup
   by Judy Hopkins and Nancy J. Martin
A Dozen Variables
   by Marsha McCloskey and Nancy J. Martin
Back to Square One
   by Nancy J. Martin

SAVING, STORING, AND HIDING

Storing the leftover fabrics that result after making each quilt can sometimes pose problems. I store any large pieces of fabric with my yardage of the same color family. Oftentimes there are extra pieces, strips, or bias squares cut to specific sizes. I store the strips in plastic containers marked with the width of the strip, for example, 1", 1½", 2½", and so on.

I store bias squares in plastic bags, according to their cut sizes; for example, 2¼" x 2¼", 2½" x 2½", 3" x 3", and so on.

Having these precut units on hand allows you to make a pillow or small wall hanging when you need a gift in a hurry. Allow these units to accumulate if you want to make a larger project.

Ocean Waves

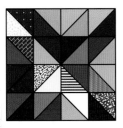

BLOCK A
8" X 8"

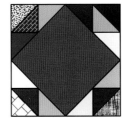

BLOCK B
8" X 8"

HALF BLOCK A
4" X 8"

HALF BLOCK B
4" X 8"

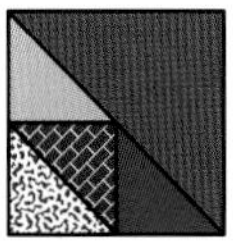

CORNER BLOCK
4" X 4"

Finished block size: 8" x 8"

Ingredients

	Small Wall Hanging	Large Wall Hanging	Double
Finished Size	48½" x 48½"	64½" x 64½"	80½" x 96½"
Block A	4	12	31
Block B	5	13	32
Half Block A	8	12	18
Half Block B	4	8	14
Corner Block	4	4	4
No. of 2½" x 2½" Bias Squares	160	360	800
2⅞" x 2⅞"*	32	72	160
6⅛" x 6⅛"	5	13	32
9¼" x 9¼"**	1	2	4
4⅞" x 4⅞"*	2	2	2
Inner Border			
1¼"-wide strips from background	4	6	8
Middle Border			
2"-wide strips from contrasting fabric	4	8	9
Outer Border			
6¼"-wide strips from background	6	8	10
Backing			
Yardage Required	3¼ yds.	4¼ yds.	7½ yds.
Seam Orientation	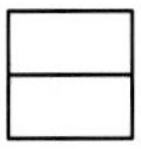	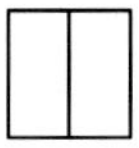	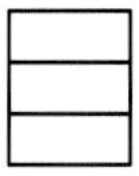

*Cut each square once diagonally to make 2 triangles.

**Cut each square twice diagonally to make 4 triangles.

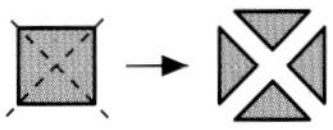

Block Assembly

NOTE: Refer to the cutting chart for the number of blocks to make for your quilt size.

1. For Block A, arrange and sew together bias squares following the piecing diagram.

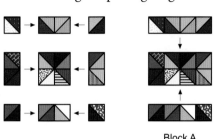

Pressing

Block A

2. For Block B, arrange and sew together the pieces, following the piecing diagram.

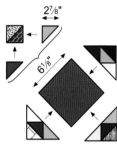

Pressing

Block B

3. For Half Block A, arrange and sew together bias squares, following the piecing diagram.

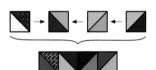
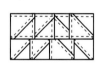

Pressing

Half Block A

4. For Half Block B, arrange and sew together the pieces, following the piecing diagram.

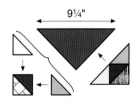
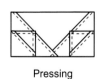

Pressing

Half Block B

5. For Corner Block: Arrange and sew together the pieces following the piecing diagram.

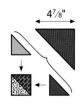

Corner Block

Pressing

Quilt Top Assembly and Finishing

1. Referring to the diagram for your quilt size, arrange and sew the blocks, half blocks, and corner blocks into rows. Press the seam allowances in opposite directions from row to row. Sew the rows together.

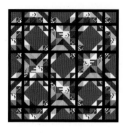

Small Wall Hanging

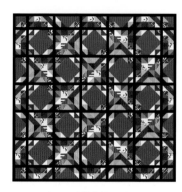

Large Wall Hanging

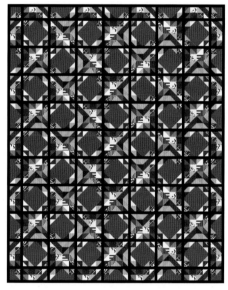

Double

2. Add 1¼"-wide inner border, 2"-wide middle border, and 6¼"-wide outer border, following the directions for borders with straight-cut corners on page 102.

3. Layer the quilt top with batting and backing; baste. Quilt as desired, or follow the quilting suggestion on page 115. (See "Finishing Techniques" on pages 102–109.)

4. Bind the edges with bias strips of fabric.

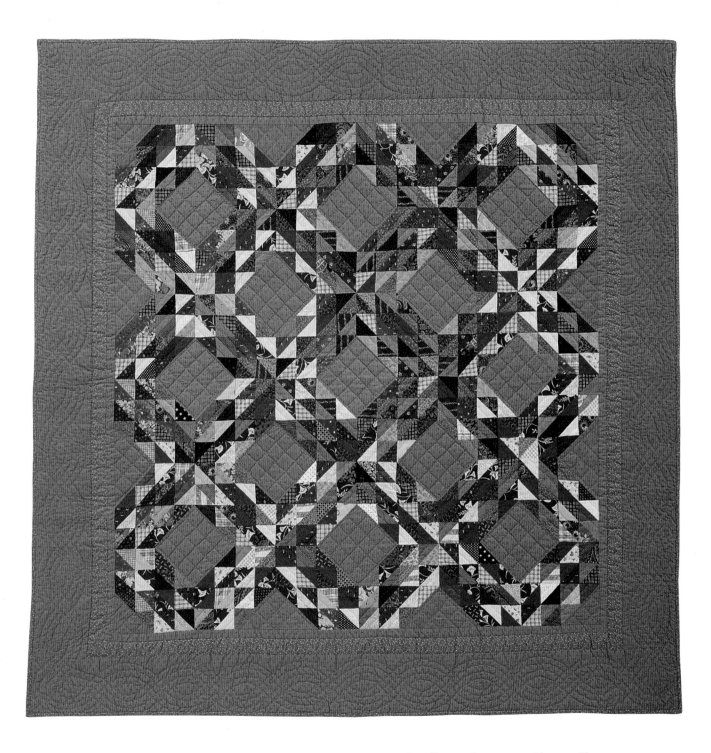

OCEAN WAVES, pieced by Nancy J. Martin, 1990, Woodinville, Washington, 64$\frac{1}{2}$" x 64$\frac{1}{2}$".
Leftover bias squares from several years of quiltmaking found their way into this Ocean Waves quilt.
The double-pink background effectively ties together the many scraps.
Quilted by an anonymous quilter. (Collection of That Patchwork Place, Inc.)

Scrappy Star

Finished Block Size:
12" x 12"

Ingredients

	Pillow	Wall Hanging	Crib	Twin	Double/Queen
Finished Size	12" x 12"	32" x 32"	44" x 56"	68" x 92"	92" x 92"
No. of Blocks	1	4	12	35	49
Setting	1	2 x 2	3 x 4	5 x 7	7 x 7
No. of 2½" x 2½" Squares					
Bias Squares	16	64	192	560	784
Light Squares	16	64*	192	560	784
Dark Squares	4	16*	48	140	196
Inner Border					
No. of 1½"-wide strips	–	4	6	10	10
Outer Border					
No. of 3¼"-wide strips	–	4	6	10	10
Backing	13" x 13"	33" x 33"	46" x 58"	70" x 94"	94" x 94"
Yardage Required	–	1 yd.	2¾ yds.	6 yds.	8⅝ yds.
Seam Orientation	–	–			

*The quilt in the photo on page 99 shows a variation of this pattern. One dark square replaces one light corner square in each block. The blocks are joined so that the dark corners meet, forming a secondary star pattern at the center of the quilt.

Block Assembly

1. Assemble blocks, following the piecing diagram.

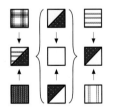

Make 4

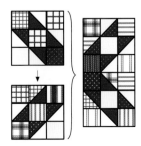 

2. Join the blocks into rows. Sew the rows together.

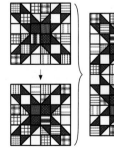

3. Add 1½"-wide inner and 3¼"-wide outer borders, following the directions for borders with straight-cut corners on page 102.
4. Layer the quilt top with batting and backing; baste. Quilt as desired, or follow the quilting suggestion on page 115. (See "Finishing Techniques" on pages 102–109.)
5. Bind the edges with bias strips of fabric.

SCRAPPY STAR, pieced by Nancy J. Martin, 1994, Woodinville, Washington, 32" x 32".
Leftover bias squares from indigo and white quilts are combined in this crisp little wall hanging.
Quilted by Donna K. Gundlach, Olympia, Washington. (Collection of That Patchwork Place, Inc.)

Friendship Star

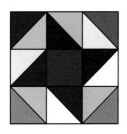

Finished Block Size:
6" x 6"

Ingredients

	Pillow	Wall Hanging	Crib	Twin	Double/Queen
Finished Size	16" x 16"	34" x 34"	34" x 52"	58" x 70"	82" x 82"
No. of Blocks	4	25	40	99	169
Setting	2 x 2	5 x 5	5 x 8	9 x 11	13 x 13
No. of 2½" x 2½" Squares					
Bias Squares	32	200	320	792	1,352
Dark Squares	4	25	40	99	169
Pieced Border					
No. of 2½" x 2½" Squares					
Bias Squares	16	40	52	80	104
Dark Squares	12	24	30	44	56
Backing	17" x 17"	35" x 35"	36" x 54"	60" x 72"	84" x 84"
Yardage Required	–	1⅛	1¾	3⅞	5¼
Seam Orientation	–	–	–	⊟	⊞

Assembly

1. Assemble blocks, following the piecing diagram.

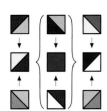 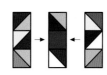

2. Join blocks into rows. Sew the rows together. Arrange the bias squares and dark squares around the edges of the quilt top. Place a dark square at each corner. Sew the squares into rows. Sew the rows to the quilt top.

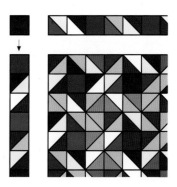

3. Layer the quilt top with batting and backing; baste. Quilt as desired, or follow the quilting suggestion on page 115. (See "Finishing Techniques" on pages 102–109.)

4. Bind the edges with bias strips of fabric.

FRIENDSHIP STAR, pieced by Nancy J. Martin, 1994, Woodinville, Washington, 34" x 52".
A pattern of dark and light fabrics emerges when leftover bias squares are divided into light and dark values in this
Friendship Star block. Inspired by an original design by Paulette Peters of Elkhorn, Nebraska.
Quilted by Donna K. Gundlach, Olympia, Washington. (Collection of That Patchwork Place, Inc.)

ADDING BORDERS

Borders can be used to frame and soften a busy design. They are also helpful in enlarging a quilt to fit a standard-size bed. It isn't always necessary to have a border on a quilt, however. Many antique quilts made from scraps have no borders, since continuous yardage was scarce and expensive.

Straighten the edges of your quilt top before adding borders. There should be little or no trimming needed for a straight-set quilt.

NOTE: *If you prefer to make borders with mitered corners, refer to page 79.*

To find the correct measurement for straight-cut border strips, always measure through the center of the quilt, not at the outside edges. This ensures that the borders are of equal length on opposite sides of the quilt and brings the outer edges into line with the center dimension if discrepancies exist. Otherwise, your quilt might not be "square" due to minor piecing variations and/or stretching that occurred while you worked with the pieces. If there is a large size difference between the two sides, it is better to go back and correct the source of the problem rather than try to make the border fit and end up with a distorted quilt.

Straight-Cut Corners

The easiest border to add is a straight-cut border. This method has been used on almost all the quilts with borders in this book. You will save fabric if you attach the border to the longest sides first, then stitch the border to the remaining two sides.

1. Measure the length of the quilt at the center. Cut two of the border strips to this measurement.

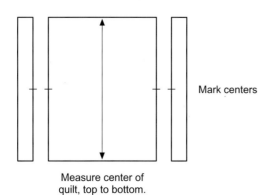

Measure center of quilt, top to bottom.

If you cut borders on the crosswise grain, you may need to piece strips together before adding them to the quilt.

TIP: The seam will be less noticeable and stronger if it is pieced on an angle. You may need additional fabric to do so.

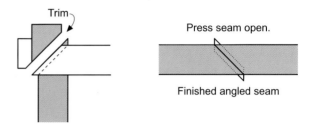

Trim

Press seam open.

Finished angled seam

2. Mark the centers of the border strips and the quilt top. Pin the borders to the sides of the quilt, matching centers and ends and easing or slightly stretching the quilt to fit the border strip as necessary.
3. Sew the side borders in place and press the seams toward the borders.
4. Measure the center width of the quilt, including the side borders, to determine the length of the top and bottom borders. Cut the border strips to this measurement, piecing strips as necessary. Mark the centers of the border strips and the quilt top. Pin borders to the top and bottom of the quilt top, easing or slightly stretching the quilt to fit as necessary.

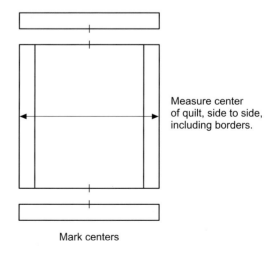

Measure center of quilt, side to side, including borders.

Mark centers

5. Sew the top and bottom borders in place and press the seams toward the borders.

MARKING THE QUILTING DESIGN

Whether you machine or hand quilt, you'll need to mark a design to be quilted on the quilt top, unless you are stitching in-the-ditch, outlining the design ¼" away from all seams, or stitching a grid of straight lines, using ¼"-wide masking tape as a guide.

- To stitch in-the-ditch, place the stitches in the valley created next to the seam. Stitch on the side that does not have the seam allowance under it.

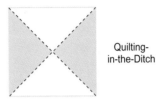

Quilting-in-the-Ditch

- To outline a design, stitch ¼" from the seam inside each shape.

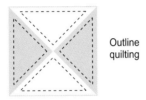

Outline quilting

- To mark a grid or pattern of lines, use ¼"-wide masking tape in 15" to 18" lengths. Place strips of tape on a small area and quilt next to the edge of the tape. Remove the tape when stitching is complete. You can reuse the tape to mark another area.

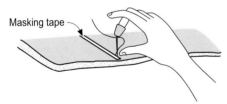

Masking tape

CAUTION: Don't leave tape on a quilt top for an extended length of time; it may leave a sticky residue.

To mark complex designs, use a stencil. Quilting stencils made from durable plastic are available in quilt shops. Use stencils to mark repeated designs. There is a groove cut into the plastic, wide enough to allow the use of a marking device. Just place the marker inside the groove to quickly transfer the design to the fabric. Good removable marking pencils include Berol silver pencils, EZ Washout marking pencils, mechanical pencils, and sharp regular pencils. Just be sure to draw lines lightly.

Always test any marking device on a scrap of fabric for removability.

Use a light table to trace more intricate designs from books.

To make your own light table:

Separate your dining-room table as if adding an extra leaf. Then place a piece of glass, plastic, or Plexiglas® over the opening. (I use the removable glass from a stormdoor for safety's sake, because there is a frame around the edge of the glass.) Have the glass (or glass substitute) cut to fit your table at a glass shop, if desired, and frame or tape the edges to avoid cut fingers. For an additional fee, you can have glass edges finished to eliminate the sharp edges.

Once the glass is in place, position a table lamp on the floor beneath it to create an instant light table. If your table does not separate, two card tables or end tables of the same height can be pushed together to create a support for the glass.

BACKING

For most quilts larger than crib size, you will need to piece the backing from two or more strips of fabric if you use 42"-wide fabric. Seams can run horizontally or vertically in a pieced backing, as long as the fabric isn't a directional print. Avoid the temptation to use a bed sheet for a backing, as it is difficult to quilt through. Cut backing 3" to 4" larger than the quilt top all around. Be sure to trim away the selvages where pieces are joined.

Plan to put a sleeve or rod pocket on the back of the quilt so you can hang it. (See page 109.) Purchase extra backing fabric so that the sleeve and the backing match. Once you know the finished size of your quilt, refer to the following illustrations to plan the backing layout and to determine how much fabric you'll need.

Sometimes the backing fabric is a little too narrow for a 45"-wide quilt. Pieced backs are fun to make, and they can be the answer to this annoying problem.

For the upper quilt in the photo below, the checked backing was slightly narrow, so I trimmed a 6"-wide strip from one lengthwise edge. I then took leftover

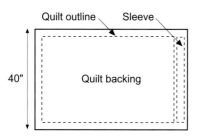

One fabric length:
For quilts up to 40" width or length
Example: 60" (length or width) + 18" (½ yd. for trimming and sleeve) = 78" (2⅛ yds.)

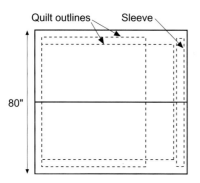

Two fabric lengths:
For quilts up to 80" width or length
Example: 2 x 100" (length or width) = 200" + 27" (¾ yd. for trimming and sleeve) = 227" (6⅓ yds.)

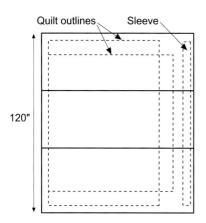

Three fabric lengths:
For quilts up to 120" width or length
Example: 3 x 100" = 300" + 36" (1 yd. for trimming and sleeve) = 336" (9⅓ yds.)

segments, bias squares, and partial blocks from the quilt front and pieced a 4"-wide strip. I stitched this pieced strip between the two sections of navy blue checked fabric, giving the backing a decorative touch while solving a problem.

You can also use scraps of fabric from your sewing stash, piecing them together to form a backing large enough for your quilt top. This is most effective when you use some of the fabrics that were used on the front of the quilt.

BATTING

There are many types of batting to choose from. Select a high-loft batting for a bed quilt that you want to look puffy. Lightweight battings are fine for baby quilts or wall hangings. A lightweight batting is easier to quilt through and shows the quilting design well. It also resembles antique quilts, giving an old-fashioned look.

Polyester batting works well, doesn't shift after washing, and is easy to quilt through. It comes in lightweight and regular lofts as well as in a fat batting, or high loft, for comforters.

Cotton batting is a good choice if you are quilting an old quilt top. This batting must be quilted with stitches no more than 2" apart.

Dark batting works well behind a dark quilt top. If there is any bearding (batting fibers creeping through the top), it will not be as noticeable.

LAYERING AND BASTING

Open a package of batting and smooth it out flat. Allow the batting to rest in this position for at least twenty-four hours. Press the backing so that all seams are flat and the fold lines have been removed.

A large dining-room table, Ping-Pong table, or two large folding tables pushed together make an ideal work surface on which to prepare your quilt. Use a table pad to protect your dining-room table. The floor is not a good choice for layering your quilt. It requires too much bending, and the layers can easily shift or be disturbed.

Place the backing on the table with the wrong side of the fabric facing up. If the table is large enough, you may want to tape the backing down with masking tape. Spread your batting over the backing, centering it, and smooth out any remaining folds.

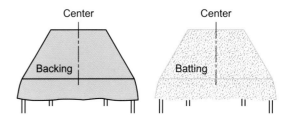

Center the freshly pressed and marked quilt top on these two layers. Check all four sides to make sure there is adequate batting and backing. Stretch the backing to make sure it is still smooth.

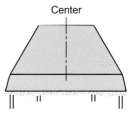

The basting method you use depends on whether you will quilt by hand or machine. Safety-pin basting is generally used for machine quilting, while thread basting is used for hand quilting.

Thread Basting

Starting in the middle of the quilt top, baste the three layers together with straight pins while gently smoothing out the fullness to the sides and corners. Take care not to distort the straight lines of the quilt design and the borders.

After pinning, baste the layers together with a needle and light-colored thread, so the thread color won't bleed onto the quilt. Start in the middle and make a line of long stitches to each corner to form a large X.

Continue basting in a grid of parallel lines 6" to 8" apart. Finish with a row of basting around the outside edges. Quilts that are to be quilted with a hoop or on your lap will be handled more than those quilted on a frame; therefore, they require more basting. After basting, remove the pins. Now you are ready to quilt.

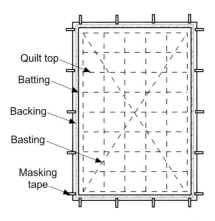

Quilt top
Batting
Backing
Basting
Masking tape

Pin Basting

A quick way to baste a quilt top is with size 2 safety pins. They are large enough to catch all three layers but not so large that they snag fine fabric. Begin pinning in the center and work out toward the edges. Place pins 4" to 5" apart.

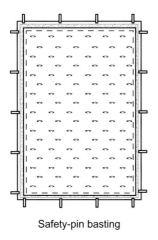

Safety-pin basting

Use long, straight pins along the outside edge to hold everything in place. Place pins perpendicular to the edge, 1½" to 2" apart.

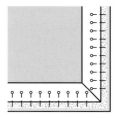

HAND QUILTING

To quilt by hand, you need quilting thread, quilting needles, small scissors, a thimble, and perhaps a balloon or large rubber band to help grasp the needle if it gets stuck. Quilt on a frame, a large hoop, or on your lap or a table. Use a single strand of quilting thread not longer than 18". Make a small, single knot at the end of the thread. The quilting stitch is a small running stitch that goes through all three layers of the quilt. Take two, three, even four stitches at a time if you can keep them even. When crossing seams, you might find it necessary to "hunt and peck" one stitch at a time.

To begin, insert the needle in the top layer about 1" from the point you want to start stitching. Pull the needle out at the starting point and gently tug at the knot until it pops through the fabric and is buried in the batting. Make a backstitch and begin quilting. Stitches should be tiny (eight to ten per inch is good), even, and straight; tiny will come with practice.

When you come almost to the end of the thread, make a single knot ¼" from the fabric. Take a backstitch to bury the knot in the batting. Run the thread off through the batting and out the quilt top; then snip it off. The first and last stitches will look different from the running stitches in between. To make them less noticeable, start and stop where quilting lines cross each other or at seam joints.

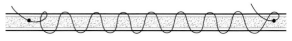

Hand quilting stitch

MACHINE QUILTING

Machine quilting is a good choice for those who have little time and need to finish their tops in a hurry. It's also a practical choice for baby quilts or other items that will need lots of washing.

Machine quilting works best on small projects; it can be frustrating to feed the bulk of a large quilt through a sewing machine.

Use a walking foot or even-feed foot (or the built-in, even-feed feature, when available) for your sewing machine to help the quilt layers feed through the machine without shifting or puckering. This type of foot is essential for straight-line and grid quilting and for large, simple curves. Read the machine instruction manual for special tension settings to sew through extra fabric thicknesses.

Walking foot
attachment

Curved designs require free fabric movement under the foot of the sewing machine. This is called free-motion quilting, and with a little practice, you can imitate beautiful hand quilting designs quickly. If you wish to quilt curved designs with your machine, use a darning foot and lower the feed dogs while using this foot. Because the feed dogs are lowered for free-motion quilting, the speed at which you run the machine and feed the fabric under the foot determines the stitch length. Practice running the machine fairly fast, since this makes it easier to sew smoother lines of quilting. With free-motion quilting, do not turn the fabric under the needle. Instead, guide the fabric as if it were under a stationary pencil (the needle).

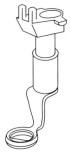

Darning foot

Practice first on a piece of fabric until you get the feel of controlling the motion of the fabric with your hands. Stitch some free-form scribbles, zigzags, and curves. Try a heart or a star. Then practice on a sample block with batting and backing. Make sure your chair is adjusted to a comfortable height. This type of quilting may feel awkward at first, but with a little determination and practice you will be able to complete a project with beautiful machine quilting in just a few hours.

Keep the spacing between quilting lines consistent over the entire quilt. Avoid using complex, little designs and leaving large unquilted spaces. For most battings, a 2" or 3" square is the largest area that can be left unquilted. Read the instructions enclosed with the batting you have chosen.

Do not try to machine quilt an entire quilt in one sitting, even if it's a small quilt. Break the work into short periods, and stretch and relax your muscles regularly.

When all the quilting has been completed, remove the safety pins. Sometimes it is necessary to remove safety pins as you work.

BINDING THE EDGES

My favorite quilt binding is a double-layer French binding made from bias strips. It rolls over the edges of the quilt nicely, and the two layers of fabric resist wear. If you use 2¼"-wide strips, the finished width of this binding will be ⅜".

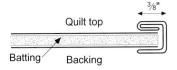

Quilt top
Batting   Backing

Double-Layer French Binding

The quilt directions tell you how much fabric to purchase for binding. If, however, you enlarge your quilt or need to compute binding fabric, use this handy chart:

Length of Binding	Fabric Needed
115"	¼ yd.*
180"	⅜ yd.
255"	½ yd.
320"	⅝ yd.
400"	¾ yd.
465"	⅞ yd.

*It is a good idea to purchase ½ yard of fabric instead of ¼ yard so the bias strips will be longer and the binding won't have as many seams.

Determine the distance around your quilt and add about 10" for turning the corners and for overlapping the ends of the binding strips.

After quilting, trim excess batting and backing even with the edge of the quilt top. A rotary cutter and long ruler will ensure accurate straight edges. If the basting is no longer in place, baste all three layers together at the outer edges. If you intend to attach a sleeve or rod pocket, make one now to attach with the binding. See page 109.

1. Cut 2¼"-wide bias strips as shown on page 22.
2. Stitch bias strips together, offsetting them as shown. Press the seams open.

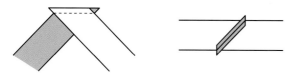

3. Fold the strip in half lengthwise, wrong sides together, and press.

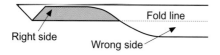

4. Unfold the binding at one end and turn under ¼" at a 45° angle as shown.

5. Beginning on one side of the quilt, stitch the binding to the quilt, using a ¼"-wide seam allowance. Start stitching 1" to 2" from the start of the binding. Stop stitching ¼" from the corner and backstitch.

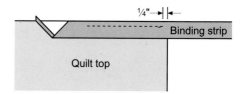

6. Turn the quilt to prepare for sewing along the next edge. Fold the binding away from the quilt as shown, then fold again to place the binding along the second edge of the quilt. (This fold creates an angled pleat at the corner.)

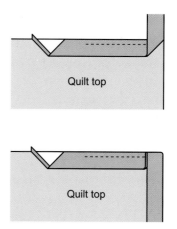

7. Stitch from the fold of the binding along the second edge of the quilt top, stopping ¼" from the corner as you did for the first corner; backstitch. Repeat the stitching and mitering process on the remaining edges and corners of the quilt.

8. When you reach the beginning of the binding, cut the end 1" longer than needed and tuck the end inside the beginning. Stitch the rest of the binding.

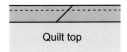

Quilt top

9. Turn binding to the back side, over the raw edges of the quilt, and blindstitch in place, with the folded edge covering the row of machine stitching. At each corner, fold the binding as shown to form a miter on the back of the quilt.

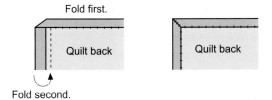

Fold first.

Quilt back

Quilt back

Fold second.

QUILT LABELS

It's a good idea to label a quilt with its name, the name and address of the maker, and the date on which it was made. Include the name of the quilter(s) if the quilt was quilted by a group or someone other than the maker. On an antique quilt, record all the information you know about the quilt, including where you purchased it. If the quilt is being presented to someone as a gift, also include that information.

To easily make a label, use a permanent-ink pen to print or legibly write all this information on a piece of muslin. Press freezer paper to the back of the muslin to stabilize it while you write. Press raw edges to the wrong side of the label. Remove the freezer paper and stitch the label securely to the lower corner of the quilt. You can also do labels in cross-stitch or embroidery.

QUILT SLEEVES

If you plan to hang your quilt, attach a sleeve or rod pocket to the back before attaching the binding. From the leftover backing fabric, cut an 8"-wide strip of fabric equal to the width of your quilt. You may need to piece two or three strips together for larger quilts. On each end, fold over ½" and then fold ½" again. Press and stitch by machine.

½"   ½"

Fold the strip in half lengthwise, wrong sides together; baste the raw edges to the top edge of the back of your quilt. These will be secured when you sew on the binding. Your quilt should be about 1" wider than the sleeve on both sides. Make a little pleat in the sleeve to accommodate the thickness of the rod, and then slipstitch the ends and bottom edge of the sleeve to the backing fabric. This keeps the rod from being inserted next to the quilt backing.

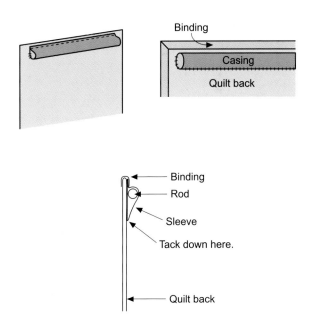

Binding

Casing

Quilt back

Binding

Rod

Sleeve

Tack down here.

Quilt back

Quilting Suggestions

Evening Star
Directions begin on page 33.

Wonderful World
Directions begin on page 38.

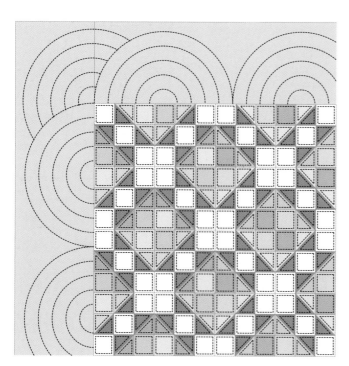

Contrary Wife
Directions begin on page 36.

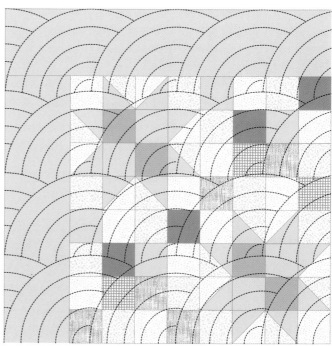

Road to Oklahoma
Directions begin on page 42.

Ribbon Block
Directions begin on page 45.

Goose in the Pond
Directions begin on page 55.

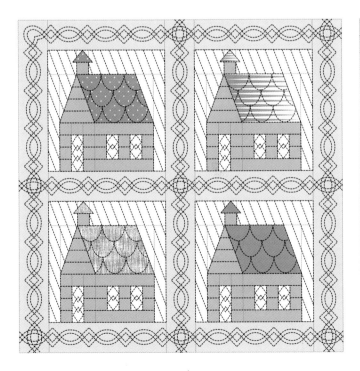

Old Country Church
Directions begin on page 50.

Dutchman's Puzzle
Directions begin on page 58.

Free Trade
Directions begin on page 61.

Grape Basket
Directions begin on page 64.

Mystery Block
Directions begin on page 67.

Star and Chain
Directions begin on page 70.

Chimneys and Cornerstones
Directions begin on page 73.

Double Cross
Directions begin on page 76.

Christmas Wreath
Directions begin on page 86.

Love Chain
Directions begin on page 80.

Ohio Star
Directions begin on page 84.

Four by Four
Directions begin on page 90.

Ocean Waves
Directions begin on page 95.

Scrappy Star
Directions begin on page 98.

Friendship Star
Directions begin on page 100.

That Patchwork Place Publications and Products

4", 6", 8", & metric Bias Square® • BiRangle™ • Ruby Beholder™ • ScrapMaster • Rotary Rule™ • Rotary Mate™ • Bias Stripper™
Shortcuts to America's Best-Loved Quilts (video)

Many titles are available at your local quilt shop. For more information, send $2 for a color catalog to
That Patchwork Place, Inc., PO Box 118, Bothell WA 98041-0118 USA.

☎ Call 1-800-426-3126 for the name and location of the quilt shop nearest you.